Tried, Tested & Being Approved

The Ernie Berry Story

Ernie Berry

ISBN: 978-0-578-03865-0

Printed in the United States of America

Please visit: www.ernieberry.com

NOTE: All scripture references are taken from the 1611 translation
of the King James Bible

Table of Contents

Acknowledgments

I would be remiss in expressing gratitude to any one person prior to acknowledging the guiding grace of God, without which this story would never have been played out with such a positive outcome.

The second tier of accolades is due to my parents, whom share responsibility in establishing a firm foundation from where I could ambitiously pursue life's ultimate purpose. First, my mother who fought tooth and nail from the first day that she knew that she had a child with special needs to guarantee him a fair shot at life; first by relentless prayer and then in equal fervor in action. She has constantly kept me grounded in the importance of honesty, openness, integrity, and humility. Secondly, my father who taught me the importance of hard work and persistence. His supervision also made many of the projects cited in this book come to fruition.

A special thanks and gratitude are due to Greg Powell, my lifetime mentor and friend, as well as Todd Gage, one of my closest friends in life. I believe these two individuals have been placed in my life from on high as high-octane cheerleaders who have always motivated me and encouraged me to strive for greatness.

Last but certainly not least, thank you to everybody who has graciously contributed in easing the barriers obstructing my life's journey. From the entrepreneurs who invented the various Voice/Text software programs, to the individuals who have given me even just one ride across town on a snowy day when the buses were running late, permitting me to make it to class or to an appointment on time, to the people involved in the production of this book. Regardless how big or small the action, collectively this group of people too great to number contributed to my life in ways that they may never realize.

Prologue

I have never had the desire to write a book because throughout my academic studies I had read so much terrible literature that I do not want to contribute to the ever-growing list of meaningless texts. I have also concluded, through extensive research into many fields, that unapplied knowledge is worthless when compared with wisdom gleaned from experience. Rather than engaging in a mere academic exercise, I wish to articulate the experiences I have endured that have imparted far greater wisdom in my life than the thousands of books I have read and digested in pursuit thereof.

Anybody engaged in an objective pursuit of the truth and the ultimate meaning of life will find themselves in front of the cross of the Lord Jesus Christ, recognizing the God of the Bible as the Supreme Creator, knowing the end from the beginning and seeing Him (the Holy Spirit) as our intercessor upon the Son's ascent to the Father after His resurrection. I offer minimal persuasive theological arguments, philosophical explanations, or convincing biblical commentary to validate this claim, but rather allow the compelling story of my life to serve as a testament to the aforementioned claim.

I can unequivocally affirm to the reader that if the revelations of a real relationship with the Trinity of the Bible had not been instilled in me at an early age I would not have had motivation, determination, and perseverance to:

- read more than twenty-five hundred books
- win a chess tournament
- place in weight-lifting competitions
- be recognized for scholastic proficiency at the state level in both high school and college
- work in Washington, D.C.
- host a radio show
- write for a newspaper
- run for city council and state representative
- purchase a five-thousand square foot house for a dollar and restore it
- work in the administration level for the city of Toledo
- graduate with a Master's degree and two post-graduate certificates

All this was completed by the age of twenty-four.

If it weren't for the God factor, in addition to being blind and virtually crippled, paralyzing depression would have certainly been the number one malady prohibiting me from accomplishing any one of the aforementioned items.

This manuscript is intended to minister and edify a multitude of people in different situations. First, to the unbeliever, my greatest desire is that it will assist you in the realization that salvation through Jesus Christ is the only way to heaven. To the person enduring an affliction of any kind, I hope it serves as an encouragement of the brevity of our condition and how the present condition cannot be compared to the glory that awaits us if we are faithful to the end. May it encourage and inspire all Christians to maximize their purpose in the body of Christ and push hard toward the finish line. Lastly, to everybody, I hope this work relays the message that miracles still happen and as the footsteps of the Messiah draw closer, the supernatural will be more evident than in any other time in the history of the world.

Part 1

Two Cups of Affliction

There are different kinds of abilities in the body of Christ: no disabilities exist. This is not a statement directed towards stimulating false optimism amongst those in unfortunate situations, but rather to encourage those who find themselves in less than desirable circumstances. It may be through no fault of their own, but that the unique purpose of God in their life can and will be expressed through a life that seems ravaged to the point of obsolescence.

"For no temptation that is uncommon to man has befallen you and God will always provide a way out" (1 Corinthians 10:13). One should not allow himself to fall into a mindset where circumstances are unique and insurmountable; it's merely a matter of degrees. Some people have more burdensome crosses to bear than others. Preoccupation with looking about to gauge the size of others' burdens may cause them to lose sight of how small theirs is.

"God has not allowed anyone to be tempted beyond the point of which they can bear, but has also provided a way of escape" (1 Corinthians 10:13). It is so easy to get caught up in finding an escape in the midst of a tenuous, fiery trial, yet when one persists in pressing forward he will discover the end is just beyond the field of vision. In hastening the journey through the trial by keeping continuous forward motion, a person also prevents himself from being utterly consumed by the flames. Stagnation is the only way in which Satan paralyzes people to ineffectiveness by pain, worry, fear, bitterness, negative emotions, etc., but in pressing forward, God will be provoked to shield and protect those who are in His will from even a stitch of clothing being singed.

Furthermore we are to, "count it joy to face trials of all kinds, for the perfecting of our faith, for faith brings about endurance, which leads to perseverance" (James 1:2-3). When we are subject to trying situations, faith, which is connected to one's spirit, is strengthened and purified. This adjusts our perspective of hope that is attached to our soul. When one's spirit and soul are working in complete harmony, the result is a supernatural encounter of the God-kind.

Even though God works incredible good out of unspeakable tragedy, it doesn't mean He orchestrates the tragedies. Don't assume that God's utilization of adversities means that He needed them to accomplish His purpose. Grace doesn't depend on suffering to exist, but where there is suffering grace will be found in

6

many facets.   It's not so important to determine the source of suffering, whether it be directly from Satan or merely the result of living in a fallen world. What is important is the response through the suffering.

I have been stricken with two debilitating conditions. From a physical standpoint these were designed to render me ineffective and hinder me in my life's purpose.   I was born with a visual impairment and when I was twelve-years-old, I was afflicted with an acute neurological disorder which brought unpleasant, residual effects and nearly paralyzed my legs. The combination of both of these maladies oftentimes endangered my physical body to the point where direct intervention from the supernatural realm was necessary in preventing serious injury, or worse. One of the most notable of these instances occurred during a hiking expedition on a trail in Hocking Hills, Ohio.

The steep, tree-root riddled paths wound up and down hilly regions in the middle of the forest, often on ridges overlooking scenic valleys below. These trails are a nice walk for the average nature lover, but for someone who has limited appreciation for aesthetics, and whose equilibrium has been severely compromised, the trek can be dangerous. After stumbling a few miles over the terrain I found myself tripping down a steep decline and heard some people yelling for me to, "Stop!" This was a difficult command for me to adhere to, due to the lack of control that I had over my legs. I felt myself fall and start to slide. When I finally came to a stop I was just inches away from a cliff that dropped hundreds of feet to the forest floor.

According to my best friend, Todd Gage, who witnessed the entire incident, "It was the first time that I knew that there was a

God who assigned guardian angels to protect people because there was no other explanation as to why Ernie didn't fall off the cliff." He further recalled that when he looked at my parents faces' he saw calm expressions as if incidences like that were a normal occurrence. I assure you that incidences with no quantifiable explanations, otherwise known as miracles, have occurred consistently throughout my lifetime. I have incorporated many of them into this volume, but omitted the majority lest this book be many more pages in length.

Chapter 1

Beating Blindness

For somebody to be classified as legally blind, they have to have visual acuity that *is less than* 20/200. The base line for measuring normal visual acuity is 20/20. If the top number is less than twenty, and the bottom number remains at twenty, a person has a greater than average visual acuity. However, if the numerator remains at twenty, while the denominator exceeds twenty, the measurement indicates that the person can see at twenty feet with approximately the same clarity as what somebody with 20/20 vision sees the same object expressed in the denominator. My acuity since birth has remained constant at 20/600, three times the threshold to be regarded as legally blind. I can see objects at 20 feet that someone with normal vision can see from 600 feet away.

It's very difficult to relate how images are projected to my brain through eyes that have been in a state of optic atrophy since birth, even with the measurement system previously explained. It is not uncommon for somebody to ask me if things appear blurry or small. I chuckle while I explain that since I've never known 20/20 vision I have little conception of what is "blurry." When we arrive to the inevitable color question, where an inquiry of how well I can see color is asked, I respond by saying that, "Although I can see all the colors of the spectrum, I can't distinguish between all of them." Black and white is no problem, but yellow, orange, red, green and brown all appear indistinguishable. Likewise blue and purple appear the same, and all the earth tones appear to be a separate color group unto themselves. When it comes to colors it's a matter of degrees; yes, I do see colors, but nowhere near what somebody with "normal" color perception visualizes the color spectrum as.

Distance is a similar scenario. "Can you see twenty or thirty feet in front of you?" I can actually see the sun and the moon, but a car bearing down on me twenty feet away is not in my range. There is no clear-cut way to describe how it is to see or not to see with 20/600 vision. It is best stated by my mother, "Ernie sees just enough to be dangerous!"

A common fallacy that people have about somebody with vision loss is that they are automatically gifted with other senses that are immediately amplified to compensate for the loss of vision. When I was being trained to cross streets independently as a young boy, the only way to determine traffic flow was by acute listening. At first this was tenuous and it would take three or four light changes before I was confident it was safe to cross.

After crossing hundreds of streets in this way, it became second nature to the point where I felt comfortable relying on my hearing to jay-walk a six lane, superhighway, which is not advisable in any situation. As I said earlier, I see just enough to be dangerous.

I honed acute listening skills by listening to speech at normal rates of one hundred twenty words a minute. Then I gradually increased it to six hundred words a minute. Eventually from listening to books at a high rate of speed, I developed an ability to listen to multiple information streams simultaneously after years of multitasking and practice. I did similar training in touch to where I can quickly run my fingers over an object and detect an imperfection invisible to the naked eye. Furthermore, I developed my sense of smell to the point that I can smell smoke from a further distance than a person who relies on their ability to see a fire. I often advise people that I can hear, feel, and smell better than they can see, not because of a particular gift, but through years of discipline in perfecting these senses.

There have been blessings which have allowed me to capitalize on these traits, such as an arsenal of adaptive computer software components that have facilitated advanced knowledge in a plethora of fields which might not have been possible if I had 20/20 vision and relied solely on visual learning. My complete collection of amazing machinery consists of a Close Circuit Television (CCTV), which allows images to be magnified up to thirty-six times, ZoomText software which allows magnification of computer based content and a voice synthesizing program that converts text on a computer to audio and a Kurzweil program that allows me to scan any physical documentation and convert it to audio by the computer.

Rounding out this high tech software is a cell phone which

can receive a complete text file from my personal computer and then convert the text to audio. This gives me access to a virtual library on my cell phone. In addition to this feature, if I need to read something on the run, I can take a picture of it and the phone will convert the captured text in the camera window to audio. I can also take a photograph of something printed in a foreign language and it will be converted to English in audio. I can also take a picture of currency and it will tell me what denomination I am holding in my hands. It will even read my contacts, calendar, and other cell phone features, such as global positioning system and the internet.

By using all of these programs in conjunction, I can listen to any book, at any time, at a rate of six hundred words a minute. This allows a God-given gift to be manifested in my life—the ability to comprehend and retain an enormous quantity of information without having to re-read anything. This allowed me to read over twenty-five hundred full-length books and graduate from college with multiple advanced degrees by the age of twenty-four. In essence, God replaced at an exponential rate more than what the enemy had been permitted to steal.

If a person is looking for instant restoration of things Satan has stolen only, then they may be disappointed. When they place a demand on the cross of salvation, which also yields healing, they sometimes learn lesson during the process of restoration. It is dangerous to claim that because a person does not receive a creative miracle, their faith is sufficient for salvation but not for healing. In a tragic accident in which a horse trampled Deborah Shamborah, she should have died according to medical accounts. However, she survived and everything was restored except for her full vision. Some could view this as an incomplete creative miracle.

In place of this, however, God allows her to see the spirit realm with her physical eyes. Although I have not been granted this ability to the extent as Deborah Shamborah, I certainly have a heightened sensitivity to the supernatural realm due to the lack of physical distraction which otherwise would be a hindrance if my vision was completely restored. This is not a justification for not receiving a creative miracle due to lack of faith, but rather an explanation as to why some people are not immediately healed when prayed for. I do believe that God will restore my sight here on earth for a sign, wonder, and miracle, but not before the purpose of this time of impairment has been fulfilled.

It was no walk-in-the-park overcoming a visual impairment. One afternoon walking home from elementary school, a group of teenagers threw eggs at my head and naturally, since I couldn't see them, I failed to duck. It didn't hurt me, so I continued on home. A subsequent walk home found me stepping off the sidewalk along a busy intersection and falling hip-deep into a hole along the curb that a city crew had been excavating to uncover a man-hole. After climbing out and continuing down the same street and stepping off the next corner, the same thing happened. Being aware at this point that more corners on that street were under construction, I crossed and took an alternate route. When I arrived home, I cheerfully informed my mother of the day's events.

This optimistic attitude, in conjunction with focusing on the positive and not the negative attributes in a given situation, accounts for my overcoming inclination. For instance, when I started riding the bus as my primary means of transportation, instead of dwelling on the countless times that I was left stranded by a bus that blew past me when I didn't stand up in time, I'd focus on how inexpensive it was taking the bus in relation to buying a car, insurance, fuel and maintenance. Instead of growing weary of all the commotion caused by immature school kids, I thought of the many more fascinating and interesting people that I had an opportunity to meet and converse with on public transit.

Chapter 2

Down but Not Out

A potential dialogue between God and Satan probably occurred in heaven prior to my existence similar to the following. Satan said, "I know you gave me permission to strike Ernie with blindness, but he will overcome that affliction through physical adaptations and to truly try him, I'll need permission to strike him additionally with a greater affliction that mere mortal man cannot ease."

God may have answered in a similar fashion as He did upon Satan's proposition of Job, "Very well, but see that my servant Ernie will be faithful to the end!"

This rendition of what occurred prior to my existence is

probably the most suitable explanation as to why Satan was given license to afflict me with two unrelated, rare conditions that are so statistically improbable that a single person would develop both, that a Satanic assault is the only satisfactory explanation.

Just prior to my twelfth birthday, I was stricken with an acute neurological attack that landed me in a wheelchair for two weeks. Through intense therapy I regained my motor skills enough to utilize a walker, a cane, and then eventually walk unassisted for a brief period of time. That victory was short-lived as I relapsed to the point where I had to rely heavily on a cane again. The condition itself left my leg muscles in such a weak state that the only way walking was possible was through a subconscious effort of my brain to send signals to my leg muscles to continuously stay in a state of contraction, thereby artificially strengthening them to the point where baring weight on them was possible.

This was the first physical drawback to my condition, as unrelenting spasms are very uncomfortable. As my leg muscles continued to atrophy due to years of abnormal muscle activity, the spasms became more intense to compensate for the degradation. In short, the most adequate simile that I can draw without belaboring the issue is that it's like a constant "charley horse" sensation throughout my lower extremities which gradually intensifies with time. A remedy to reduce the spasms came in the form of one of the most potent neuro-relaxants in pharmacology. Unfortunately, this ended up having more negative consequences than benefits. For this reason, I was thrust into a very "nerve-racking" decision. I had to break a seven-year dependence on this very toxic drug despite my neurologist's advisement that I'd have, "bone-shattering spasms and other painful side effects" if I didn't stretch the timetable of coming off the medication over years.

The physical barrier brought on by the spasticity in my legs was the lesser of insurmountable obstacles brought into my life at twelve years of age. The physical discomfort was mentally blocked to the point where my entire pain tolerance was greatly increased. The rehab efforts required consistency, intensity, and mental endurance to press through the workouts to offer my physiology the greatest opportunity to regain what had been lost. However, the psychological and emotional challenges were not as easy to overcome.

Unlike my visual impairment, where I had no idea what it was like to see from the 20/20 perspective, I was fully aware of how it was to play sports, run, walk, and even stand in one place uninhibited. In essence, I knew what I was missing. Prior to the onset of this condition I played football, baseball, basketball and other sports with no inhibitions. After the position of the ball or other objects were brought to my attention, either by a teammate's audible notification or by the audible noise that the ball made as it flew through the air, I kept up with the rest of the team. I ran cross country track and even competed in triathlons. My father ran beside me and identified where the divots and trees were to avoid collisions. This active lifestyle abruptly stopped about halfway through my eighth grade year with a hospital stay. At that moment a sizable portion of my athletic ability was stripped away from me instantly.

Being in a family were athletics and physical activity were an imperative, I found myself in a position where not only was the ability gone, but my psychological and emotional response was crucial in handling my circumstance. It is emotionally devastating for a young pre-adolescent, who was used to enjoying all of the activities that bring normal children satisfaction, to suddenly find himself in a situation where physical limitations render him incapable of the previous level of engagement. Negative emotions ran rampant and were amplified when my physical symptoms increased and my condition digressed despite maximum rehabilitation efforts. I had to make the decision to not allow my emotions to dictate my attitude, lest I develop depressive tendencies and my life be squandered.

After fending off the emotionalism I decided to live life with an extreme mentality, pursuing everything as aggressively as I did my rehabilitation. The pursuit of a humanly insurmountable condition led to the hurtling of obstacles with ease that I might never have attempted if I were not in pursuit of physical wholeness that were not attainable through my own willpower.

Spastic paraplegic neuropathy proved to be an even tougher challenge to overcome than blindness and will ultimately require a major creative miracle to lick the problem once and for all, but in the interim, minor miracles provide the strength to carry on.

There are two ways miracles supernaturally manifest in the natural realm. The first is an unquantifiable spiritual intervention that transcends all physical laws. These types of miracles occur when a physical agent threatens something that has a divine supernatural protective covering. A classic illustration is when John G. Lake, a famed missionary to Africa in the early 1900s, evangelized in places where the bubonic plague decimated the indigenous population without physical safeguards. He had physicians analyze the reaction of the virus when placed directly on the flesh of his hand. To everybody's amazement, the virus cells instantly died as soon as they came in contact with John G. Lake's skin. This phenomenon can only be explained by an invisible spirit realm, which gives license and authority over the natural realm. Natural quantifiable, empirical evidence guarantees that any exposed flesh that the bubonic plague comes in contact with inevitably results in infestation and death. However, when one understands, as John G. Lake did, that the physical realm is controlled either by good or evil supernatural forces, and that the root and seed of the mechanism through which Satan brings death and destruction is cursed, the ensuing result is the immediate death of a virus that has a 100% infection rate according to all natural laws.

The second way creative miracles are manifested are by utilizing the methods taught by the Word of God to cure what are thought to be incurable conditions by medical science. Perhaps the most notable of this type is found in the case of Jordan Rubin, who was a 6'1" tall, 180 pound college athlete. At nineteen, he developed eighteen different incurable diseases, including Crohn's disease, and soon his body was emaciated to 104 pounds. After consulting world renowned physicians of all types and generating thousands of dollars of debt, one of his acquaintances called across the nation and said he had the solution, "If you eat as the Bible specifies, you will be healed!"

He flew to meet his friend to carefully plan a diet in exact accordance to scripture. After months of doing this, his conditions started improving and in a few years, he went from 105 pounds to a healthier condition than he had been prior to the onset of his illness. Furthermore, all eighteen of the "incurable" conditions were eradicated. Jordan Rubin went on to found the "Garden of Life" corporation, a whole food supplemental company whose mission is to offer everybody products and nutrition plans that reflect the biblical dietary plan delineated in the scriptures. The physical ailments that struck Jordan Rubin were agents influenced by evil spiritual forces sent to rob him of his health and attempt to kill him. God could have easily performed an instantaneous creative miracle by cursing the root and seed of all eighteen illnesses, but His prescription was already captured in the text of the Bible for thousands of years and God opted to perform the miracle through dietary change. This is as impressive as an instantaneous healing and illustrates that satanic assaults can be thwarted through quantifiable physical responses.

Equipped with the understanding of how supernatural miracles of healing were made manifest in this physical world after the Garden of Eden, where the natural and supernatural were divorced, I began a two pronged approach to my healing. The driving force behind my efforts was, "faith, if it hath not works is dead" (James 2:17). Regardless how a miracle would manifest itself in my life, there would not be any such manifestation unless I took action stimulated by faith.

With the onset of the neurological condition, I instituted a regiment of prayer where I spoke to the spiritual forces causing my situation and commanded them to "let go of my life." When I said it, I fully expected that the condition would instantaneously dissolve just as the bubonic plague germs would dissolve when the power of God made contact with them in John G. Lake's situation. I supplemented these daily prayers by the prayers of those who I esteemed as spiritual authority figures. Despite exercising the necessary faith entailed in receiving a creative miracle none was immediately forthcoming, much to my disappointment.

Rather than permitting frustration to consume my thoughts, I acted on a scripture that encouraged the active pursuit of the solution to my problem through natural measures and in doing so a miracle was guaranteed -- gradually or otherwise.

Since I was aware that the instructions God relayed to Moses for the Israelites on how to eat was in itself a divine guide to health and wellness, our entire family adjusted our diets accordingly to reflect the divinely inspired nutrition plan of the Bible. In addition, we pursued more intense nutritional cleanses to purify our bodies of toxins consumed through foods contaminated with man-made pesticides and alterations, as well as contaminants in the environment ingested through breathing or through the skin. I felt tangible, physiological benefits from adopting biblical nutritional habits. However, I did not achieve the desired elimination and reversal of my digressive condition through these nutritional practices.

After observing a resurgence of the negative effects left by the viral infection, my parents and I sought medical advice in determining a cause and solution for my condition. Justified by the notion that God uses the medical establishment in utilizing knowledge, wisdom, and understanding of the human anatomy which He created, my parents and I determined that neurologists might be the mechanism through which God might manifest a miracle. We consulted three local neurologists prior to traveling to the world renowned Cleveland Clinic and Johns Hopkins University in Baltimore, Maryland to meet with experts in neurology. Through these visits we 'learned' that the diagnosis of Spastic Paraplegic Neuropathy was incurable; the spasticity would become more acute with time and the symptoms were best treated with baclofen. The most effective method of treatment in relieving symptoms proved to be very rigorous exercise routines performed on a daily basis to offset the spasticity, stress, and negative emotions that accompany such unrelenting conditions.

In the final analysis, coping is the most suitable way to describe my approach in dealing with the situation. Exercise was the primary way in dealing with the physical, mental, and emotional effects. Benign cynicism, harmless sarcasm, and humor employed in discussing real and serious circumstances were supplemental mechanisms in dealing with an otherwise depressing situation. Physicians, nurses and other hospital personnel often asserted that, "It is unheard of to have a patient with your type of condition who is so upbeat and optimistic." That always facilitated opportunities for me to explain my source of hope and joy as being the confident expectation of good, and it is only a matter of time before all these negative experiences are turned around for something good. In fact, the stamina in enduring these hardships provided the drive, motivation, and perseverance in attaining goals not attempted if I was not driven by a problem which couldn't be transcended through physical means. I've chronicled many of these accomplishments in the succeeding chapters in illustrating how God can create miracles through circumstances that Satan has orchestrated to defeat a person without having to perform a miraculous physical healing first.

Part 2
Living Life to the Fullest!

Chapter 3

A Prosperous Family

Mother: A Conservative, Hard Working Foundation

Rebecca Barto was born in 1959 on a dairy farm in Green Springs, Ohio, the last of seven children, into a fifth generation of farmers. She was raised conservatively with her parents teaching her good sound Christian morality and ethics. The Bartos attended a First Missionary church in the small town of Clyde where they would make the half hour trip every Sunday morning and night and the Wednesday midweek service from the countryside regardless of the weather conditions.

It was a simple life growing up in the four bedroom farmhouse, built in 1906. Being the youngest, her two brothers and her oldest sister were married and moved out of the house. The old saying that "Kids to a farmer are worth their weight in gold" was true in that the responsibilities and expectations placed on the children were great in helping to keep the dairy farm operational. Becky had to rise before school and feed the calves and horses among other chores. After school there was more hard and tedious work. It seemed there was no end. Saturdays were the same, filled with backbreaking work that had to be done in the bone-chilling cold or blazing heat and all climates in between. Minimal chores were done on Sundays; it was the Lord's Day and reserved for church service, afternoon scripture reading, and rest. It was not all hard work; there was much time for play at the lake in the summer time and in the snow in the winter. However, there was an ethic that children were to work as hard as they played and vice versa. This portrait comprised Becky's upbringing until she was eighteen years old and had to choose a path to pursue in continuing her life's journey.

Her eldest sister Joanne went to college to be a teacher and later married Merle Hurt, a former Air Force pilot. They settled on a farm a few miles outside of Fremont, Ohio. Joanne taught at an elementary school for thirty-five years before retiring.

Gene and Larry, her older brothers, married and started farming land in keeping with the Barto tradition. Larry built a house next door and Gene built a house on the outskirts of Tiffin. Each would become very successful farmers, hardworking and devout just as their father, Oral. Gene raised pigs and Larry took over the family's dairy herd for several years before switching it to a pig farm. Both moved on to solely planting corn and soy beans. When Gene retired he was inducted into the National Farmer's Hall of

Fame. Both Gene and Larry invented numerous innovations to the agricultural sciences and have a legacy of hard work and persistence leading to success and prosperity.

Doris helped with the daily milking of the cows; she rode and showed horses. She later sought employment at a factory that makes cabinetry. This is the place she later retired from. She eventually married Bob Dull.

Bonnie, the middle of five sisters, married her high school sweetheart Jerry. He became a teacher and taught in the Old Fort School District where the Barto children had attended school. They moved into a house situated on a ten acre plot of land and raised two children. Debbie grew up, became a teacher, and moved out to Fresno, California to teach.

When Becky graduated from Old Fort High School in 1977, she decided to pioneer new ground and become the first in her family to cut a nitch for herself in the medical profession. To achieve these means, she decided to study biology in her undergraduate studies at the University of Toledo. She thought that this route was advantageous in leading to formal training in the medicinal sciences upon graduation and acceptance into med school. She was well on her way in attaining this goal, a dean's list student, diligent in her studies, but then she was introduced to a young man by the name of Pete Berry during a meeting at The Church in Toledo.

Father: Patient Persistence

Pete Berry was born on November 11, 1952 and raised in a small three bedroom house situated on Utah Street on the East Side of Toledo. He was the sixth of eight brothers and sisters. It was a typical rearing for a child born into a large Catholic family, living in an urban area, in the midst of the baby boom. The family wasn't wealthy by any means, so the early bird got to wear the clean socks. This was desirable due to the constant outside activity which left clothes in a perpetual state of foulness.

Over 100 kids lived in a one block radius in his neighborhood. The television only received one channel between the hours of 5:00 PM and 8:00 PM. Unless a sporting event was on that particular station during those hours, the kids were out playing basketball, baseball, and doing whatever else kids did to pass the time. Often baseball teams were comprised of a dozen or so players, all playing at once, in a field consisting of an eight foot wide concrete alley, with a broomstick for a bat and a ten cent rubber bouncy ball. The kids had to postpone the game if a passing car wanted to get through. Such were the rules of the concrete playground.

Pete as well as his preceding and succeeding brothers and sisters attended Good Shepherd Grade School and he attended Cardinal Stritch High School where he was taught in the authoritarian, corporal style of the Nuns of Notre Dame.

"Yes ma'am," "No ma'am," "Do as I say when I say it with no hesitation," and "If you step out of line, there's the rod of correction." If you didn't like it, there was certainly no telling parents for fear of maximizing the pain and suffering through the 2x4 of correction at home.

This was a typical upbringing in the Roman Catholic tradition. Work hard, go to mass, raise your children with a rod of iron, send them to a school that reinforces those values, and they'll grow up to do the same. This was not true for Pete; he always had a suspicion of something more. It didn't compute -- hard work, hard pursuit of fleshly desires remedied by talking to a man in a box every Sunday morning claiming to be the only median through which men could communicate with God. This did not lead to lasting fulfillment. There had to be something else; there had to be an answer other than line that he was indoctrinated with.

As with every person who is objectively seeking the truth, he found it at the Cross of Christ Jesus. He was working as a floor buffer at the Chrysler plant in Perrysburg, Ohio where he cleaned a spot welder's work area. George Loux was joyful and happy all the time. What is more, he was always reading a book and counseled people on Thursdays. Pete approached him one day to inquire as to the source of all his happiness, to which the gentleman responded by pointing to the book Pete had observed him reading on many occasions. He provided Pete with a copy of the Bible and advised him that the answer to all of life's questions were contained therein. He went on to encourage Pete to begin reading in the Gospel of John and to continue reading the remainder of the gospels.

After about a week, Pete approached him and inquired of the concept of salvation that was talked about in the Bible and how he desired to be saved. He paused and looked at Pete and responded, "Pete, you're not ready to be saved." Pete was utterly confused and continued to read his Bible, after all it said that the gift was open to all, and now somebody's telling him he was unqualified. Two more weeks went by and Pete approached the gentleman in his work station and inquired again, which generated the same response, "You're not ready yet." Pete was still confused, however encouraged at the same time because this time he had said "Yet," which meant that there may be some sort of time component involved in the process. Before he approached him a third time, Pete prayed and read his Bible for an entire month and felt that there's no way that he'd be denied a third time. Again the response was, "You're not ready yet," which puzzled Pete beyond belief. He did not understand why somebody who spent hours counseling, witnessing, and sharing the gospel with a person for close to two months was capable of denying him three times.

Pete poured himself into his Bible, spending every waking hour reading, praying, and seeking answers for the dilemma he found himself in. The next time Pete inquired about salvation he was not to be denied; the burden was too heavy on his conscience. If this man prohibited Pete from receiving salvation, then how was it any different than the Catholicism that did absolutely nothing for him? But still there had to be something genuine behind the brand of salvation that George's countenance demonstrated. After another month Pete's inquest was finally met with a positive response and at last Pete was led in the sinner's prayer.

The deliberate withholding of salvation through the delay in praying the sinner's prayer occurred for two reasons. First, the man of God observed an indication that Pete's heart was not truly ready and only when the persistence, sincerity, and unrelenting attitude was evident did the man of God see that Pete was truly ready to receive salvation. Secondly, a character trait was instilled in Pete through that experience which was passed down to the next generation to somebody who would be prohibited from obtaining the promises of God for a time, but through the relentless, persistent pursuit of the things of God realized the full blessing of God which is bestowed on those who are tried, tested, and proved.

A Successful Family

Upon tying the knot, my parents moved into a modest, three-bedroom house on the East Side of Toledo where they raised a family and have resided for twenty-eight years. My father was hired into the local bus service after being laid-off from the Chrysler plant. My mother, staying true to her foundational roots became a stay-at-home mom while raising their four children. She taught aerobics and exercise classes at the local YMCA during her child rearing years, which provided a recreational outlet for the children as well as a means of relieving stress. When the youngest was junior high age and the boys had graduated high school, she finally joined the workforce as a teacher. She was hired as a part-time tutor for students with learning disabilities by Toledo Public Schools. This soon developed into a full-time position.

Abram, the oldest child, was born on December 17, 1982. He had exceptional coordination even as a child, walking by the age of nine and a half months, his athleticism was evident while a toddler. He was very athletic growing up and into high school, where he graduated with sixteen varsity letters, four in each sport of soccer, cross country, wrestling and track. After graduation, he entered the Air Force where he anticipated being assigned to a Special Forces unit until they disqualified him on account of color-blindness. He trained to be a fire fighter and served two tours of duty in the Middle East. He was discharged after four years of service and was then hired into a federal fire department in Seaside, California. There he provided fire services for the metropolitan area as well as for the state when they were in need of assistance in extinguishing the forest fires every summer. In the

32

spring of 2009, he moved closer to home when he was hired into the fire department on Wright-Patterson Air Force base in Dayton, Ohio.

I was the second child, coming seventeen months after my brother. In jest, my parents proudly proclaim that God has blessed them with seven children; Ernie, Abram, Ernie, William, Ernie, Janelle and Ernie. I'll reserve my commentary for the ensuing chapters, however, I will say that if every facet of my life was transcribed, several volumes would have to be printed to contain it.

Four years passed before my parents had a third child. My brother William was born on September 26, 1988. He was born with a rare heart defect known as Epstein's anomaly which meant he had a defective left ventricle -- so defective that the doctors were unable to maneuver a heart catheter through his left ventricle chamber. He underwent a closed heart surgery at two months of age which was basically to buy time for him to grow and possibly for new medical advancements to be made. There was not a corrective procedure for his defect – only a compensatible one. My brother William died at 40 months of age, shortly after undergoing his second heart surgery. God's goodness and grace was increased in my family's lives as we learned to lean on Him and one another to make it through, to count the blessings for each day we had with William on this earth and to look in anticipation of our reunion in glory.

Janelle arrived two years after William's birth and has developed into a God-fearing woman after the tumultuous teenage years. She grew up with the normal exposure to sports and participated with a considerable amount of physical ability as her oldest brother, but not quite as much heart, so high school and club sports were the extent of her athletic career. She was diagnosed with dyslexia while in junior high, a fairly common neurological disorder where neuropathways from the eye to the brain are affected causing letters and numbers to appear backwards.

Thankfully my mother was astute at addressing educational inhibiters and began working with my sister on proper study methods. This has reduced the problem to near non-existence. As college time neared for Janelle, she decided to combine her passion for horses and the overcoming spirit over disadvantages which are prevalent in her family. She decided to study business management and plans to eventually operate a facility that uses horse riding as a means of therapy for developmentally delayed people.

Chapter 4

Supernatural Provision

My parents eagerly awaited the birth of their second son in the bedroom of their house on Oswald Street in Toledo, Ohio. All the preparations had been made, the contractions were coming more frequently and the midwife was on hand ready to catch the new bundle of joy. After two hours of intense labor, my mom finally delivered an eight pound, fifteen ounce baby boy. They had consecrated their first born to the Lord by bestowing a Biblical name on him. Their second born carried his grandfather's name to the third generation - - Ernest Walter Berry III.

As with many newborns, I made my entrance into this world raising a racket and refusing to be comforted by anyone other than my mother, screaming and crying for most of my awake hours. My mother attributed my crying as retribution for being blessed with such a content first child. Before long, my mother had a suspicion that there was an underlying issue provoking such unrest. My crying was incessant; I rarely napped for longer than a half hour at a time. She became more attentive in trying to deduce what was the matter. She had already noted to our family doctor that my eyes jiggled back and forth, but he had assured her there was no need for alarm. She began to think that the issue was most likely sight related as I refused to be comforted unless she was holding or touching me.

She grew more and more convinced as she observed my scooting and crawling patterns. I felt in front of me to make sure the path was clear. Even still the doctor refused to agree, stating that even if I were visually impaired, determining visual perception was difficult prior to the ability to communicate with a youngster. By the age of two when I finally began walking I had already knocked out my top two front teeth in separate accidents. My mom says this was a blessing in disguise because prior to that I had a weekly bloody lip. My mother's concern that my visual limitation was more acute than the doctor admitted was solidified by my clumsiness. I tripped over and ran into objects that a toddler with normal sight avoided. As my ability to walk increased, so did the safety issues as I moved faster and ran into immovable objects with greater and greater force. It was becoming a necessity to determine actual visual acuity in attaining glasses.

Since my mother was reared with the understanding that education was critical in developing the intellect, especially in young children, she took it on herself to home school my brother and me when he was in kindergarten and I in pre-school. She was still unclear of how much I could actually see as the handful of eye doctors we visited were unsuccessful in getting me to read charts. Nevertheless this did not deter my mother from instilling the foundational building blocks of education in me at a young age. She took the time to explain concepts to me if I didn't visually see her demonstrate a concept.

My parents made the decision to send my older brother and me to a private Catholic school down the street when my younger brother was born with the heart defect when I reached kindergarten age. This only lasted one year when my mother realized that there was no way for the first grade teacher to spend the individualized time I required. My brother and I once again were home schooled for the next three years. My parents ordered large print textbooks, as well as books on tape to facilitate my learning. Even though the text was a very large font, I had to squint and struggle to see every letter. It was incredibly frustrating for her and me, but my mother worked with me for hours after my brother was complete with his subjects to assure that I not only completed my lessons, but fully understood them.

My parents took me to see a low vision specialist when I was seven years old. He projected the usual eye chart on the wall in an attempt to have me read it to no avail. Then he handed me a miniature card with sentences of various sizes and a high-powered magnifier and asked me to read a sentence. I squinted and strained to read the first sentence and any subsequent ones he asked. He switched to a different powered magnifier and asked me to read a sentence. Even though he'd changed the order, I was able to read them from memory after only seeing the first word.

This worked well until my mother suggested he give me a new card with varying sentences as I was not moving the magnifier but recalling the sentences from memory!

By the end of my visit he managed to have me read some of the eye charts on the wall with one of the hand held magnifiers, the first ophthalmologist to accomplish that. He determined that my visual acuity was 20/600, which essentially means that for me to see an object at relatively the same clarity that a person with 20/20 vision sees an object when they are standing 600 feet away from it, I have to be 20 feet away from it. My vision readings from the various eye exams from nine months of age to this point ranged from 20/60 to merely "reading fingers."

Since a doctor was now able to pinpoint my exact visual acuity, my parents were in the position of having to investigate and utilize the various support mechanisms in place for parents of children with visual impairments to maximize my opportunity of becoming successful throughout and after childhood.

Their quest took us to the State School of the Blind in Columbus, Ohio during their annual retreat for families with blind children. The campus and school was specifically designed to teach and train visually impaired children from kindergarten to twelfth grade in the proficiencies that lead to independence and success after graduation. The classes were equipped with the latest state of the art adaptive hardware and software components that ease the barriers to intellectual development. The school also housed culinary and home economic classes to teach blind people to cook and learn independent skills in daily living. The classes were taught by instructors who were visually impaired themselves, or equipped with the expertise in training visually impaired youngsters in the respected classes. I never was sent as a student to the school on account of the distance and because my parents did not want to place me into a setting where I was only with other blind and visually impaired children. My parents were, and are, staunch in their belief that normal social development was contingent upon peer interaction with non-impaired students. Despite this, we eagerly looked forward to the summer retreats to learn of the newest developments in rehabilitation technology. The teaching staff occupied students with the fancy talking computers and magnifiers, while the parents assembled for different motivational, counseling, and support sessions where they discussed the different challenges and obstacles in rearing children with visual impairments.

My parents made a decision after the first conference that, although they were not going to send me to Columbus for formal education, they were obligated to offer me the adaptive equipment to optimize my learning potential. They discovered the closest school to offer what I needed was Elmhurst Elementary, a Toledo Public School, that has a self-contained classroom for visually impaired and blind students. An essential component of mainstreaming a child with a disability that effects their education at any level is the IEP (Individualized Education Plan) in which the administrators, teachers, parents and the student discuss the barriers in receiving an equal education and how to mitigate those challenges. Accommodations such as extended time in taking tests, note taking by other students, and, of course, adaptive computer software were all discussed. Prior to the provision of any of the proposed remedies, a psychological evaluation had to be undertaken to deem whether my cognitive capacity justified such expenditures.

My parents made an appointment for the necessary evaluation. As I walked into the room, the evaluator was already seated and ready to go. He didn't waste much time getting started; holding up a pen, he asked me what color it was. The pen wasn't even visible, never mind what color was it, so I did what any nine-year-old does in my situation and responded, "The pen is blue." He then proceeded to push a paper in front of me and asked me what was missing to which I responded, "From what?" He replied, "From the pencil." By this time I was concerned that he was the one who needed the psychological evaluation. Asking questions which relied on visualization to determine a visually impaired person's intelligence was like asking an elephant to fly. At any rate the questions continued, centering on visual prompts. I eventually asked him if he knew that I was visually impaired. He responded he did, but urged me to answer the questions to the best of my ability. So the guessing game continued until the last illustration. I left the room thinking, "I have never taken such a strange test before in my life!" My optimism soon kicked in and I thought that since all of the answers were multiple choice, maybe I guessed correctly on the majority and scored well by accident.

The test was scored and a follow-up meeting between the psychologist and my mother was scheduled; he asked my mother what she felt was the best case scenario for me, to which she responded for me to attend Elmhurst. During their discussion my mother asked the psychologist how they measured one's intelligence. When she saw the cards that had been used and the sight required to answer the questions, she dismissed the test as flawed and the results invalid. She found out later that the score assigned to me based on this test indicated that I was borderline mentally retarded.

An agreement was made that I was to be assigned to the self-contained, visually impaired classroom at Elmhurst with the opportunity to be out for regular education classes fifty percent of the time. Students from across the district were bussed to this school as it possessed a classroom equipped with many of the same devices demonstrated in Columbus. This situation offered the best of both worlds: all the necessary adaptive software at my disposal, and classes in select subjects alongside sighted peers. Plus, the visually impaired and blind students also travelled to the Sight Center weekly to further the practical skills essential to independent living.

I was nervous and excited the first morning. I rose early to get on the yellow school bus which drove all around the city picking up kids with varying types of impairments to ship them to this centralized location. This was my first experience attending school so far away from home, but I was prepared for this step of independence. I wasn't worried about having to call my mother for any reason though I knew that this was always an option, if justifiable. I arrived at school and walked into my classroom with six other visually impaired students. The teacher started passing books out in a variety of formats based on the students' needs. Two students received Braille books and Braillers, which made a "ca-chunk" noise every time a letter was embossed. Two other classmates received regular text books, as their visual impairments were correctable to the point of being able to see regular print with their thick prescription lenses. The other two and I received large print text books, which were photocopies of each page, magnified four times, causing dimensions of the books to be 16 inches by 22 inches, rather than 8 inches by 11 inches. The entire textbook was contained in three or four volumes, compared to the single volume used by sighted students.

Despite the enlarged text and my thick glasses, my nose practically brushed the page and I struggled to focus on each individual letter to form the words that extended into sentences. It took minutes for me to read a single sentence, and oftentimes it took so long that I would forget the content of the subject before reading the predicate, thus I had to reread almost everything multiple times.

I developed acute headaches almost instantaneously upon reading visually. Even with these complications, I refused learning any more than basic Braille as I insisted that "Braille was going to become obsolete" in the very near future after being introduced to the voice-text software in Columbus and at the Sight Center which was still in its infancy. Besides I enjoyed listening to books on tape and retained information more efficiently by listening rather than visualization or touch. Audible books were limited because the majority of books on tape at the libraries were novels or biographical works, rather than informational books useful to a fourth grade pupil. Even still, I listened to any audio tape that I found, regardless of the content; and eventually finding the narrator reading too slowly, I sped the tape up multiple times until it sounded like the Chipmunks were reading to me.

I took math in the specialized classroom because of the unavoidable visual conceptualization learning style requiring individualized instruction. All other scholastic classes involve me slinging my oversized books under my arm and walking down the hall to join the "normal classroom" in learning. In addition, there was a mobility instructor, Joe Negrich, who came to the class and taught me white-cane skills for all circumstances and terrains in traveling from point A to point B without jeopardizing life or limb. These sessions involved walking throughout the school using the different techniques, listening to the click-click of the cane on the floor was essential in allowing the tip to notify me of steps or obstacles.

After demonstrating an ability to navigate the inside of the school, Mr. Negrich took me outside to traverse the new barriers. Once I'd mastered the skill of listening to traffic patterns in determining the appropriate time to cross minor intersections, it was time to go onto progressively more dangerous intersections. The ultimate goal was to graduate to a point when I could negotiate all traffic situations thus making riding public transit feasible. That skill took me years to master.

As the end of my first year at Elmhurst came to a close and it came time for fifth grade scheduling, my parents were advised that two of the three mainstream class instructors felt that I would have a difficult time keeping up with the class and it was in my best interest to stay in the specialized classroom for the majority of my classes. This pessimistic projection, coupled with the advice from Mrs. Limmer that educational restraint might occur if I were not challenged through mainstreamed classes and sighted peers, caused my parents to contemplate complete mainstream education at Raymer Elementary School. Raymer offered several advantages that Elmhurst didn't; the school offered an environment of complete social and educational integration, and the school was within walking distance of my house. The major disadvantage was the separation from the specialized adaptive equipment necessary to maximize my learning potential. The equipment, theoretically, would be legally mandated under an Individualized Educational Plan, however the battle would take years. The bureaucracy possessed the appropriate documentation to write me off as being unable to benefit from the provision of maximum adaptive resources, so the minimal resource provision was justified with this report. My mother prepared for a long, uphill battle in demanding that the system provide every piece of technology to prepare her son, who she knew was cognitively gifted, in acquiring the necessary resources in preparation for a college education.

At Raymer Elementary a classmate used a carbon sheet of paper in his notebook to take notes for me in class. I took the notes home and transcribed them. Our home computer was not yet outfitted with any adaptive programs, so the font was set to a large setting, and my mother read the notes as I typed. Although I despised these sessions, as it was similar to having to listen to the prior days' lessons a second time, I noticed that my mental retention of the material was immediately heightened due to forced repetition. I soon found myself competing for the highest scores on all the tests throughout my fifth and sixth grades. Toward the end of my fifth grade year, I began studying intently for the annual Geography Bee, which the smartest girl in the school had won two years consecutively. Hundreds of questions were compiled in a booklet that was distributed to all interested competitors.

I eagerly took one home, thinking that it was an excellent opportunity to gratify my competitive nature and demonstrate my mental superiority. Besides, there was a ten dollar grand prize for Toys-R-Us! My mom suggested that the appropriate study strategy was to record her voice reading the question, followed by my giving the answer for every question. When the information was captured in audio format, I listened to the tape until questions and answers were committed to my iron-clad memory file.

Excitement festered as Geography Bee day approached because I knew if anybody was to provide remote competition for me, they must have had to memorize everything as well. The two time champion and I went head to head for round after round until I claimed the ten dollar grand prize. Over-reliance on phonetics in spelling words prohibited me from being a top contender in the Spelling Bee. Although I had an extensive vocabulary at a young age, and knew how to pronounce large words, when they aren't spelled like they are pronounced, the result is being eliminated on the very first word: "adress".

A school assembly was convened on a winter morning during my fifth grade year. The area high school orchestra exhibited their various symphonic instruments, lead by their maestro, Mrs. Oliver, in the hopes of stimulating interest amongst the young, musically inclined audience. I immediately was attracted to the sound of the violin and promptly informed my mother that I wanted to join the school orchestra. She joyously responded, hoping that dormant musical genius might manifest itself through the violin, as piano lessons were a bust. Keeping with their commitment to never dissuade me from participating in activities, and probably mixed with the stereotypical notion that children born blind have an inherent musical talent, my parents rented a violin and enrolled me in the music classes at school.

Four of us comprised the Raymer Elementary orchestra. We gathered once a week with Mrs. Oliver in the third floor music room where she taught us the appropriate techniques and form in playing our instruments. I discovered immediately that there was no possible way to enlarge the sheet music to such a size where I was able to read it from the music stand three feet in front of me. Although I was made to learn the technical aspects of written scores on the music sheets, I knew I'd never be able to use it. So like Braille, I resolved to master the minimum permissible amount, and relied on my acute hearing to take over in the actual performance. A combination of memorization and playing by ear allowed me to play in harmony with the other instruments. I enjoyed playing the violin and continued playing by ear through my junior year in high school. Although I never became the musical prodigy my parents thought I might be, I eventually worked myself up to play in the first chair violin in performances, playing solos and leading the other violinists. At best, it demonstrated the ability for a visually impaired youngster to master a musical instrument through hard work, despite being void of natural musical talent. And at least the experience satisfactorily met the credit obligations for graduating high school.

Supernatural Protection

Growing up in a very active family in conjunction with parents who did not restrain the activities of a fiercely independent, visually impaired, go-getter through protectionism, there was always the potential of imminent fatality. I only survived because of the supernatural intervention in the dispatching of a special guardian angel from the Heavenly realm to keep me around to fulfill my ultimate purpose. It can always be determined if a person poses a threat to the kingdom of darkness and is called for a higher purpose in Christ Jesus to demonstrate His power because they are targeted at a very young age by the enemy. There is a direct relationship between the acuteness of the attacks from Satan and supernatural protection sent from Heaven.

For me it all started with my mother's pregnancy, she experienced heavy bleeding during her eighth week of pregnancy with me. Carol Barrett, our neighbor, drove my mother to the doctor's office. He informed her that if she hadn't already lost the baby, she would due to the severity of the blood loss. The whispers of the Master Physician prevailed as she and my father prayed for His intervention according to His will.

Then when I was two months old I fell ill with a virus. At first my mother assumed the dissipation within twenty-four hours, but after the third day of a fever, non-stop crying, little sleep for either of us and my inability to keep any milk down, my parents decided to ask Pastor Barrett to come, pray and anoint me with oil. They noticed the sunken fontanel as Pastor Barrett laid hands on me and prayed for healing. Pastor Barrett stayed awhile to calm and encourage my frazzled parents. My mother nursed me while they visited and for the first time in three days I kept milk down! It wasn't until later my parents learned how dire my illness had been. They found out that a sunken fontanel means dehydration and for an infant as small as I was at the time, even a day could be a serious matter. There had already been two assassination attempts by Satan on my life prior to the age of one, yet my mother was filled with a supernatural peace in releasing me to the oversight of God as He would afford me more protection than she or my father could ever provide.

My parents, the Critchelys, the Gages, and the Powells were

all friends with children about the same age who attended the same church and vacationed together. Hiking trips were a part of camping and I ran ahead with the other kids. On one such trail-blazing expedition, my brother followed a bend in the trail, and I proceeded on my straight forward trajectory. I assumed the path continued forward as my brother did not warn otherwise. My feet immediately dropped out from under me and I felt myself sliding down a very steep decline. Then I stopped suddenly, suspended by an unknown object. When my parents caught up to me, they found me hanging from the hood of my sweatshirt caught on a tree root about a third of the way down a steep, cliff like, embankment with a raging creek of cascading water churning over jagged rocks.

Another near catastrophe occurred while sitting around the fire at our campsite. I was leaning forward on my folding lawn chair roasting a marshmallow. I was unaware that my chair was about to collapse and fell completely into the fire ring. I heard people screaming and I froze; getting out under my own power was impossible. My dad jumped up and quickly pulled me out of the fire. I had landed on my feet and stood for at least twenty seconds in the flames. Amazingly the laces of my shoes were not even singed, only the rubber soles of my tennis shoes were slightly melted.

These events comprised the average day, not just on camping trips but in everyday life in which the statistical probability of severe injury was so great, yet not even a scratch was sustained. There was no explanation except supernatural protection.

Despite the regularities, such as running full speed into an end table and knocking over scalding hot coffee, which should have left third degree burns yet no such casualties were absorbed, my normal rambunctious activities would find me in the bathroom on an ongoing basis while my mother put peroxide, antiseptic, and band-aids all over my body just in time for me to go back out and sustain more cuts and scrapes. I was so determined to be part of the group regardless of a few bumps and bruises. I was determined to play harder than the rest to become the best. Even if it meant catching a baseball with my nose and then running into a television with my face two weeks later, breaking my nose again and needing stitches in my lip, or falling head long down unseen concrete steps, landing squarely on my arm and breaking it, or sustaining severe frostbite after capsizing a sled after sideswiping a fence. I was determined to never allow my lack of sight to prevent me in attaining my internal desire to do everything sighted children did.

My parents bought me a bicycle when I was five years old and my father outfitted it with training wheels until I developed the equilibrium to ride unassisted. As in many other things, mastering a two wheeled bicycle was delayed. It came about a year later. Until I developed the skill, I would practice and fine tune my riding skills on a daily basis to keep pace with the rest of my friends. I had restrictions placed on how far I was able to ride on account of my age, so I was permitted to ride three houses down to the boundary line where I ran into a tree while turning around. After brushing off and hopping back on my bike, I peddled back towards the other boundary line, a few houses down in the opposite direction I had just come from. On the way down, I tried to keep the handle bars straight to keep in the center of the sidewalk. If I felt my wheels rub against the edges of the grass, I flopped over due to my inability to maintain balance or slightly turn my handle bars to redirect my bike. Crashing was inevitable, and I merely picked myself up and turned around for another round.

As my skill level increased with age and practice, I was permitted to go further, around the block and then eventually across streets to accompany others on longer bike rides. The primary challenges necessary to surmount were the trees, curbs, and other immovable objects that caused crashes when I ran into them. Resolving these dilemmas took time as I memorized the danger zones along the different routes we took. This allowed me to get around them safely. Upon running into an object, a mental note was made in avoiding it the next time. Essentially I created internal mental maps that allowed me to get from point A to point B on my two-wheeled vehicle without needing to see where I was going.

The constant variable in utilizing this form of transportation was cars. Moving cars were easily detectible because of my acute hearing, but parked cars seemingly emitted no audible noise -- until I realized that large, inanimate objects were detectible through the use of a quazi-echolocation system, much like a bat. Making an audible "ts" noise with my mouth, determination of approximately how large and where a parked car or other object was located based on the reverberations of the sound emissions was possible.

As soon as I mastered these techniques, I was unstoppable on my bicycle. I soon moved from riding on the sidewalk to the street, because riding was much faster without the worry of taking out pedestrians. I fearlessly rode down steep declines at high rates of speed and went across busy streets and across rough, unfamiliar terrain on several occasions. I was fully confident in the abilities that I'd developed to prevent serious accidents and injury, and I was aware of a supernatural protection that prohibited adverse conditions if my own safeguards failed.

In reality, the latter was more prevalent than the former in accounting for my survival through that phase in my life as there were several instances that unless an angelic presence hadn't intervened, I most certainly would have sustained fatal injuries. On one occasion I was following one of my new friends to a riding course that he claimed was, "Really cool." We quickly headed off in the direction of the high school, crossed a few busy streets, passed under a viaduct and turned into a gravel drive. He instructed me to dismount, as we had to lift our bikes over a fence.

When we scaled the fence, he informed me that, "This is a dirt bike trail," where people raced motorcycles around a track with very steep hills. He said that, "If you build up enough momentum on your bike a complete revolution on the track is possible." I thought it was a great new challenge and started off after him. Of course I didn't see the first hill, so as I started up it, I fell to the side and tore a gash in my knee. I quickly hopped up and wheeled my bike back to the start to give it another try. This time I made it to the summit, but not realizing there was a required left hand turn, I kept the handle bars straight. My bike did a nose dive and I tumbled over my handlebars.

After falling and knocking the wind out of my lungs, I thought to myself that conquest of this course required more strategic planning than I was giving it. When I regained my breath, I walked the course, carefully mapping it out in my head so I had an idea of what to expect when I mounted my bike again. I spent the entire afternoon just trying to make it over the first hill without crashing. As the sun was beginning to set, we decided that it was time to head home. My mother listened intently to my ramblings as she cleaned and bandaged my bloodied and battered knees and elbows.

I was enthralled with the challenge posed before me. That night as I lay in bed, my head raced with thoughts of how to make it around the track without crashing. I eagerly anticipated the next time an opportunity to ride arose. The next weekend, I did not find anybody to go to the track with me so I decided to make the journey myself. I spent hours that day at the track with minimal progress towards completing the circuit, but had similar results as the week before in returning home a mess.

When school let out for the summer, I made the trip daily, pressing on towards completion of my goal. After a few months of relentless pursuit of the goal, despite nearly breaking arms, legs and even my neck, I finally made it around once. The next day, I made it around twice, and then three times. Eventually I road the course and made it around as many times as I wished without crashing, serving as another insurmountable feat accomplished by a blind kid which may seem unrealistic; the impossible was made possible.

Shortly after I accomplished this ultimate feat, somebody broke into our garage and took my bicycle without asking. My parents secretly saw it as a blessing. They knew that the power of prayer would continue to cover me in an adequate level of grace sufficient enough to protect me, but they also knew that it probably wasn't a good idea to perpetually test the Lord's grace.

Technological Provision

Being enrolled in honors classes for the fifth, sixth and junior high school grades was challenging for one reason -- the deliberate withholding of technological equipment that allowed me to perform at my highest potential. Although I was performing at the top of the class without the adaptive equipment for the visually impaired, if I had unrestricted access to adaptive software, no end to my learning capability was in sight. While my mother was advocating for me to the school system to provide the computer components for me on site, my parents sacrificially saved thousands of dollars to incrementally purchase the equipment to ease the learning barrier at home.

The first piece of equipment was a close circuit television (CCTV), a video camera mounted on a platform that was situated eight inches above a tray that held a book, magazine, map, or any other two dimensional object. The image captured by the camera was transferred to a monitor posted directly on top of the camera. The camera was controlled by a series of knobs and buttons which zoomed, focused and changed the contrast of the image. The magnification capacity of the machine was six to thirty-six times with a color contrast feature that allowed a myriad of possible schemes to ease eye strain. Even with the ability to magnify images to a far greater degree than large-print text books, my visual acuity was such that I still had to be very close to the screen and squint to distinguish letters. This meant enduring headaches precipitated by the eye strain. Eventually, the evolution of the machine itself eased the cumbersome process with a larger, high definition, LCD monitor and auto-focus features. But still, utilization of only this device was restricting.

The next accessible items were two software programs which allowed me to use a computer unassisted. ZoomText, the first program, allowed me to magnify the images on a computer in much the same way as that of the CCTV, but instead of a physical document I could enlarge a word processing program, the internet, or any other computer based program. Jaws, the second program, converted the text shown on a computer to audio. This program was the first to eliminate the primary barrier to learning. By listening to material, rather than looking at it or having somebody read it to me, I was able to read anything on a computer at my own pace. Since I could adjust the voice speed, the only barrier was my brain's ability to process the information. As the ZoomText program evolved to a built-in text-to-voice synthesizer it replaced the use of Jaws – no more tinny, artificial voice to endure while listening to my books!

The Type and Speak was next in line, which was the prelude to a laptop computer. The advantage to this piece of equipment over a laptop was that it was smaller and lightweight. It allowed me to take notes in class, come home and transfer them to my personal computer. Then read them, adding or taking out content for future reference. This eliminated the need for a personal note-taker followed by my laborious transcription of the written notes on my computer while my mother read them to me. I was well on my way to complete independence.

One of the last pieces of adaptive software was a program manufactured by the Kurzweil Corporation. This program allowed me to scan books, magazines, or any paper with written material on it via a flat-bed scanner which was connected to my computer. After sending the scanned image to the computer, the program converted the text to audio and read it to me at six-hundred words a minute. The program had other features such as a dictionary and thesaurus, which allowed me to look up new words that I came across. There were also search features that were very helpful in skipping to passages containing information that I was specifically looking for, making research relatively easy.

Two things were instantaneously activated as soon as I was equipped with this arsenal of adaptive software. As soon as the laborious tedium of reading was freed and replaced by an ability to listen to literature faster than a typical individual's ability to visually read, I was able to quickly develop an ability to listen to, understand, and recite entire, full length books in the span of hours. This gift combined with a passion for knowledge, which had been starved for years, and my eccentric, competitive nature, drove me to read over a hundred books the first summer that I had this new equipment. Perhaps the most astounding thing was not so much the programs which permitted this activity, but the provision of brain capacity by God to allow me to retain most of what I read without having to listen to it more than once. Although the first few years of using the software consisted of aimlessly reading anything that I could get my hands on after my academic studies were completed for the day, a situation soon cropped up in my early teens which prompted me to exhaustively study the reason for existence and the purpose for human life.

Supernatural Impartation of Endurance

My parents attended a charismatic, pentecostal, evangelical, non-denominational church prior to my birth and throughout my childhood. One of the central doctrines of the church was that the Apostolic Age did not pass away after the outpouring of the Spirit on the first century church. They believed that not only were the nine gifts of the Spirit active and available for use, but they were to be sought after and utilized on a consistent basis by all believers.

The church elders gathered continually in prayer, fasting, and pursuit of the gifts. For this reason the church was fluent in the gifts. People witnessed supernatural manifestations of miracles and healings regularly.

To bolster expectancy of the supernatural, the church hosted traveling healing evangelists. So awesome were the works witnessed in their services, they were invited to impart their level of faith to our church. The pastoral staff notified people when a well-known, or even lesser-known, servant of Christ with a healing ministry was scheduled to be at a Toledo location. While I was young child, my parents were notified that Charles and Francis Hunter were going to be hosting a service at the East Side Sports Arena in Toledo. A large percentage of whomever the Hunters prayed for received healings: from deaf ears opening to short legs supernaturally growing to people confined to wheelchairs rising and walking, and even to blind eyes seeing. My parents took me with full expectation that I was going to receive a healing miracle. When it was our turn to be prayed for, the Hunters asked what this child needed. My parents informed them that I was born blind and needed restoration of sight. They proceeded to rebuke the blindness and, "In the name of Jesus, eyes be healed," but nothing happened.

Dozens of notorious faith healers, with documented miracles, attributing everything to Jesus' work on the cross and taking no credit themselves, came to our church throughout my childhood: Mahesh Chavda, Randy Clark, Larry Randolph, and Mickey Robinson to name a few. The so-called "Generals" in the faith healing movement who had personally been privileged to witness firsthand all of the biblical miracles, including resurrection, frequented our church. A tangible anointing, accompanied by healings and other physical signs and wonders corroborating God's presence, manifested during services. The sign of a person being healed of an ailment occurred when the speaker had a "word of knowledge," meaning they would describe a person's condition and call them out of the crowd by their name. Although I was never so fortunate to receive one of the prophetic words, I'd be the first one out of my seat as soon as they said, "Now if you have a condition that I haven't called, come up right now!" I responded in faith, always visualizing myself with twenty-twenty vision as soon as the speaker released the healing anointing over me. My faith-filled response was not limited to special speakers, I always responded with an equal level of expectation when my senior pastor had a healing word, and even outside the church walls when anybody felt prompted to pray healing over my eyes.

When I was eight years old, an international evangelist from Nigeria by the name of Cletus Bassey came to our church. I was excited as I had heard of the major miracles that occurred on a daily basis in developing countries, especially Africa. I was excited that the church was hosting an apostle who witnessed the lame walk, the dumb talk, the blind see, and the incurable cured. A portion of the blessing was bound to cross the ocean with this servant of God dispatched from a region of the world which had been currently experiencing an Izuzu Street-like Revival. I fully anticipated that this was the day when he'd say that he was going to pray for somebody in the church with a visual problem. I hurried to the front of the church. After he prayed, he conducted a quick vision check. I knew that nothing had transpired, but tried to decipher the different colors of his garment upon his request.

When he realized I hadn't received a miracle, he proceeded to say, "I have a sense that he'll be healed by the time he is twelve years old." I believed sincerely that I would be healed by the age of twelve. I didn't have an understanding of the differences between a sense, impression, and prophetic utterance, so I marked the date on my calendar and thought four more years of confinement to this condition was tolerable. Instead of the expected healing occurring prior to my twelfth birthday, I was stricken with an acute neurological condition that compounded my challenges.

I began to wonder why I was not receiving the promise of healing which those who accept salvation through Jesus Christ are privy to. I used a direct word from the Holy Spirit, "shutting the prophets' mouths," to mean whatever was hindering the healing was going to be revealed firsthand to me through my diligent inquiries. I started my quest for the answer. The answer was two-tiered. First, saying that God heals indiscriminately puts God in a box to the same degree as those on the other end of the spectrum who say that God ceased working miracles after the first century church. It is in His benevolent sovereignty to determine who is healed and who receives the gift of grace and endurance.

Secondly, in the gospel of Matthew Jesus responded to inquiries of whose sin caused the blindness in a man by saying that nobody was at fault, but so that a perfect work might be demonstrated through the healing. I held fast to this second truth, as the perfect work will be performed at the appropriate time at the discretion of a Wiser Being than I. If God healed me when I was a babe in arms, only my parents would have witnessed the event. If God healed me when I was twelve years old, it would have served as a sign and miracle for the edification of my family, friends, and church. However, as the fame of notable accomplishments by a nearly crippled blind man spreads, the perfect work will be performed in a more public arena serving as a sign, wonder, and miracle for a greater number of people than if God conducted a reconstructive miracle in accordance to my timetable.

It is my contention that the astounding accomplishments while in an afflicted condition surpass a creative miracle in that it resoundingly demonstrates a new genre of miracles being poured out in these last days. The tasks delineated in the subsequent chapters are proof that God will no longer wait to re-apportion double what the enemy has stolen after the "Job"ification process, but equip individuals to withstand and move into the double portion while subject to Satan's wrath. This unique level of grace and sufficiency will not only encourage and bless other believers, but also cause non-believers to unmistakably conclude that the source behind the overcomer is the same source from where creative miracles proceed: the cross of Christ Jesus. With this confidence, I knew that prohibition in attaining God's purpose for my life was not going to occur. I went forth with a supernatural impartation of perseverance in my life.

Chapter 5

Triumph Through Suffering

Suffering Paralysis

During the winter of my eighth grade year, I attended an overnight party which was being held at WPOS, a local Christian radio station. I stayed up all night and did what teenagers do: bean bag games, obstacle courses, kick ball, etc. My friend's parents dropped me off the next morning at my house. I went directly to bed to catch up on some sleep. I slept through the day and woke up mid-afternoon feeling a little sick. I fell back asleep expecting the rest to ward off progression of my sore throat. I woke again two hours later with a sore throat accompanied with an earache. I walked down the steps to find my mom and requested her to take my temperature and my legs gave way. I collapsed at the bottom of the stairs. I attempted to stand to my feet multiple times to no avail.

My temperature was slightly elevated, but not high enough to cause any concern. My mother gave me some Tylenol and sent me back upstairs to bed. The next day I awoke still feeling achy; my legs were still unable to bear the full weight of my body and I collapsed in a heap when I tried to stand up. I decided crawling was the best means of getting around until I kicked the bug. My temperature was slightly elevated, but there was still no cause for concern. That evening my throat continued to hurt and my ears began to throb.

On Monday morning my mother contacted the doctor and the first appointment was that afternoon. After the normal checkup -- the ear, nose, throat, and other vital checks -- the doctor informed my mom that it was just an ear infection and sent me home with a prescription for an antibiotic and instructions to get plenty of rest and fluid.

Three days passed with no relief from this condition. I spent the majority of the days and nights shivering and shaking in a puddle of sweat from the unrelenting fever. I tried with all my mental ability to focus intently on the recorded books on tape that I received in the mail, but I found it incredibly difficult to follow the plots due to my aches.

Hour after hour, I tried to convince my mom that this was not the normal ear infection cycle. She called the doctor two days later and told them that the antibiotic hadn't seemed to have any effect. We made a second trip to the doctor's and, sure enough, my ear infection had worsened. A second, more powerful prescription antibiotic was prescribed. We returned home and the misery lingered. It made the hours seem like days. After another two days of being confined to my bed, my mom called the doctor again and took me in for a third visit. Once again there had not been any improvement in my condition and the pain was growing. The doctor administered a shot of Rocephin, a potent antibiotic and sent me home again.

That night my temperature spiked to over 104.6 degrees Fahrenheit and by morning I was losing my ability to walk, and even stand. My symptoms worsened over the weekend and by Monday morning walking was no longer possible without falling every few steps. My mother, fearing a potentially fatal illness like Gillion-Barei, called the doctor again. He advised my mother to take me to the emergency room.

On our way to the emergency room, I expected that the end of my problem was near. Perhaps they'd run a test, give me a pill or two, and then I'd be better.

After I explained my symptoms to the admitting nurse, they set me in a room where a nurse came in every half hour or so to extract blood for "one more test." Then a group of four nurses came in with a gurney and told my mom and me that they were taking me for a CAT scan and X-Ray tests. They quickly loaded me aboard my chariot and whisked me away.

Shortly after I returned from these tests another group of nurses came in and told us that they were taking me for a "spinal tap." This procedure was the most unpleasant of them all. I was instructed to lie on my side and curl up in a ball as tight as I could. A doctor plunged a four-inch long needle into my spinal cord between two vertebras in my lower back. It's a good thing a nurse was holding me, preventing me from flailing around from the pain of the vampire-like instrument embedded in a very uncomfortable position in my back. They expected the analysis of the extracted spinal cord fluid to provide insight into why I was experiencing an acute case of paralysis of my lower extremities.

The doctor then advised me to lie flat on my back with my head down to prevent the brain fluid, which they were drawing out with the needle, from leaking out of the fresh puncture wound. Headaches occurred if the fluid did not stop seeping from the puncture. It was getting late and I hadn't had anything to eat since breakfast. I told the nurse how hungry I was and she brought me a tray of crunchy beef stroganoff and dried broccoli. I hardly touched it on account of my pounding head and the texture of the food.

After dinner, a nurse came in and informed my parents and me that I was to be admitted to the hospital to permit them time to find a solution for my problem. As I was being wheeled to my room, I thought to myself, "This is some earache! I can't walk, I've spent the entire day being poked and prodded, I have an excruciating headache, and now I can't even sleep in my own bed!" That hospital room was my home for the next two weeks.

I wasn't able to sleep at all the first night because of all the noise. The beeping, buzzing, and crying in the crowded pediatric ward made it impossible to sleep the first night, although it became more tolerable as the nights passed; I never was fortunate enough to get a full night's sleep. If it wasn't the noise, then it was the ear pain or the fever that kept me up. As soon as I was able to stop tossing and turning, some sort of alarm or a child's scream would jolt me awake. It was a catch-22 that governed my sleeping habits for the duration of my stay in the hospital.

By morning I was completely paralyzed from the waist down

and my legs had curled into a fetal position. After breakfast a neurologist, who had been called in for my case, came into my room. He introduced himself as Dr. Sanders then asked me questions regarding the symptoms that I was feeling. I gave him the most explicit answers a twelve year old was expected to give. Before he left, he pulled out a rubber mallet and rapped me on the elbows, knees, and chin. When he checked my knee and foot reflexes, my legs jumped and I heard him mutter, "Hyperactive reflexes as I suspected." He informed me that the nurses were taking me for more tests to shed some light on the situation. The next two weeks were a whirl of blood tests, MRIs, CAT scans, and even another spinal tap. It wasn't too long before I became thoroughly annoyed with all the tests and the frustration at the inability to determine the cause for my paralysis.

Within a few days my fever was gone, but my legs were still immobile. At this point the doctors deduced that the neurological condition was triggered by the acute sickness, probably a viral infection, which had entered my body and invaded my spinal cord. The many blood and genetic tests, as well as scans, proved to be elusive. Not a single test reflected even a minute abnormality! Even still, the doctor postulated the condition was a form of transverse myelitis, which was plausible as the onset of transverse myelitis is acute with similar results, and strikes without cause. However, my symptoms didn't completely match those of transverse myelitis, but in order to discharge patients, there must be a diagnosis and that one sufficed.

The remainder of my time spent in the hospital was filled with studying for and taking the eighth grade proficiency test, which the kids back at East Toledo Junior High were busily preparing for.

The school system dispatched a personal tutor who brought a CCTV to enlarge my material up to the hospital. She proctored the examination in a room the hospital had set up for studying. I was in the most miserable condition of my life and I still had to do school work! At least I had a good excuse when I wanted to call it quits for the day. I'd just say, "I had a spinal headache from the latest spinal tap," and that would be the end of that. That was until Mrs. Masco figured out that I was abusing the excuse. The studies gave me an opportunity to stimulate my mind in something other than wondering how long this condition was going to last.

Intense therapy sessions were crammed between tutorial sessions and medical tests. These were focused on keeping my legs in motion and loose. The ultimate goal was for me to be able to walk again with the support of a walking device of some kind. This idea served as a powerful motivating factor in my therapy sessions while in the hospital and after. With the help of steroid treatment in conjunction with a strict adherence to a stringent therapy regiment, I was able to free myself from the bonds of the wheelchair and walk with the aid of a walker two days before my release from the hospital.

I had visitors nearly every night. I especially looked forward to the visitors who played chess. The chessboard was always set up in anticipation of visits from my mentor, Mr. Powell, and my other friends. We often played well past visiting hours and only stopped when the nurses kicked them out. My junior high chess coach, Mike Bartus, came many times during my hospital stay. I had practiced with the team four days a week after school and since that was not an option for the time being, he brought the practice to me. He showed me different strategies for improving my

67

game. The biggest chess tournament of the year was just months away and I wanted to do well, so why not optimize my inability for other activities to focus on the game of chess in preparation for this tournament?

I tried to make the hospital stay as enjoyable as possible so as soon as I was well enough to start wheeling myself in the wheelchair and I was no longer hooked up to an IV, I started cruisin' the halls. Next to the doors of each room there were flipdown writing boards that the nurses and doctors utilized for medical charts. These were just tall enough for a kid in a wheelchair to pass under without being decapitated. It still made the nurses nervous and they kept yelling for me to slow down. That made me speed up to prevent being caught. Soon the confinement of the pediatric floor became more than I could bear and I decided to go down to the lobby.

I waited impatiently for the elevator, and decided to practice my wheelies. I heard the elevator "ding" and thought I had time for one more. I overdid it just a bit and flipped backwards out of my wheelchair. A nurse came off of the elevator. She helped me back into my chair and wheeled me promptly back to my room. Although I did make it off the floor a few times, my efforts were quickly thwarted because a nurse decided to play a cruel joke on me by replacing my speed chair with one that had a bum wheel.

After two weeks, I was released from my captivity with orders to undergo outpatient rehabilitation to continue strengthening my legs. My mother drove me five days a week for workout sessions with my "personal trainer," KC. Before each session he attached electrodes to my legs to stimulate them in preparation for our workout. After the shock therapy he had me walk, still leaning heavily on my walker, until my body motions told him I was worn out. He read my muscles because I never told him I was tired. He then put me in a chair and rolled me to a room where he moved my legs around because I was incapable of doing so.

This was the extent of the workouts day after day for about two weeks. Then my legs started to tighten up. "Muscle memory" was the term that KC used. My muscles and brain were finally remembering how to walk, and my muscle tone and mobility was being restored. Different exercises were incorporated into our regiment, such as riding a stationary bicycle and walking on a tread-mill to supplement my muscle memory. As these tasks became easier, building endurance, strength, and light weights were added to my workouts. KC started by having me sit on the edge of a table and he lightly held my feet while I attempted to pull my toes toward the ceiling. At first they were barely moveable, but eventually I was able to do this with five pound weights strapped around my shoes.

After a few months I wasn't relying as heavily on my walker so I asked if it was time to try a cane. We walked over to the cane room and picked one up my size. I tried to take a few steps but tripped over my foot and fell flat on my face. I immediately hopped up said I was "OK" and tried again. This time I focused with all my might and I made it about six steps before I fell. As with everything else, this feat took time.

Once I was able to walk a sizable distance without tripping, KC added an obstacle course. This consisted of a dozen small cones set up in a staggered pattern. I was expected to pass through them without knocking anything over.

To this day I don't know which caused more cones to fall --

my lack of muscle control or my inability to see the cones. In any case, the exercise soon digressed from, "Try to make it through these cones without knocking any over," to "How many cones can I not mow over?" It took four solid months of therapy to move from reliance on my wheelchair to minimal dependence on my cane. I was then released from therapy. The last piece of advice that KC offered was, "Ernie, your continued progress is directly related to how much you continue to perform these exercises we've been doing."

During my rehabilitation I was going to school half days. My mother picked up my assignments from my afternoon classes, permitting me to maintain pace with the rest of the eighth grade class and attend therapy simultaneously. Though school and therapy kept me extremely busy, I found my release in the game of chess. This was an activity where there were no boundaries; nothing was prohibiting me from advancing in skill and knowledge of the game. My rehabilitation was frustratingly slow and chess was my outlet. After a long day of school, therapy, and then more school, I'd call up a friend and break out the chess board. My chess coach came over if I was unable to make it into the school for an individualized lesson. The sessions began with setting up forced checkmate positions. My mind was at the point where I was so engrossed in the study of the game that it was not uncommon for me to see seven or even eight moves ahead. We moved on to strategies and position evaluation. I was excelling in these areas and beginning to consistently beat my coach. He told me, "Ernie you are so focused due to your hunger for the game in these recent months that you'll be unstoppable at the tournament if you don't get too confident."

70

Triumph in Chess

On tournament day in mid-May, 130 seventh- and eighth-grade students gathered in Deveaux Junior High, Toledo, Ohio to determine the 1998 Northwest Ohio Chess Champion. Mark Ryan, who had won the state championship two years back-to-back, was expected to win with little competition. The tournament was organized and played over two days with each player playing six games. Each game represented a point and a player received one point for a victory, a half point for a draw/stale mate and no points for a loss. The players who won their first round matches went on to play opponents who also won the first match. After the second round, players who won two points played each other, and those with one and a half played each other, and so on. When all six rounds were finished, whoever had the most points was declared the winner. If there was a tie between two or more players, the round in which they lost their first game determined the winner. If this also was identical, the records of each opponent that they played were taken into consideration in determining which player played the toughest opponents. This rating system established a decisive winner as well as second and third place contenders in six rounds.

Players were seeded in this tournament in relationship to how many tournaments they won in the past and what their official rating was. Since I hadn't played in many tournaments and lacked an official rating, I was seeded near the bottom of the bracket. This meant I would start off on the thirteenth table. I had no idea whether my initial opponent was a stronger or weaker player than I was. After five minutes and twelve moves, I proudly walked up to the tournament director's table to inform him of my victory. The second and third matches were nearly as swift, with my opponents making silly mistakes in the opening moves. On the car ride home, I discussed strategy with my father to prepare for the more fierce competition. My dad had spent the day scoping out the head tables while I had pummeled my opposition. He advised me to take it one game at a time. "There are three more games and you'll have to win all of them to win the tournament."

The next morning, after a brief pep-talk from my coach, I took my seat at the assigned table across from a kid I had played in the past. He was a weaker player, so I thought victory was assured. My confidence must have gotten the better of me because well into the middle game, I dropped a piece. This was too late to be giving pieces away. I was used to sacrificing pieces in practice games just for the challenge of playing from behind, but this was not the appropriate time to be gambling. Besides, he had greatly improved his game and wasn't making any mistakes. There wasn't much time to regain my focus as there were only thirteen pieces left on the board. I had to avoid exchanging pieces at all costs to maintain an effective arsenal, while forcing him to make a mistake to regain my piece. Then off in the distance, four moves ahead, I saw it, the forced checkmate. It was unavoidable; I had him. There was no way out for him. As I called checkmate I thought, "That was too close for comfort!" Jeopardizing winning the tournament by underestimating my opponents was unacceptable. The competition started heating up during round five; this was no pushover round. All the pieces were still left on the board after twelve moves. Pressure was starting to build up on two pieces in the middle of the board. I knew from prior engagements when both sides had a lot of pieces focused on the center of the board, often times a massive exchange would result leaving one person with a decisive position or piece advantage. It was my move and my option to trigger the rapid trade-off. I called adjust and proceeded to touch every piece to refresh the position distinctly in my mind. I realized immediately that there was a queen-rook fork at the end which would give me the game -- providing I didn't squander the advantage. I continued to contemplate the position in my head for five minutes so as not to overlook anything. Then I moved and quickly hit my plunger. He moved quickly and five rapidly successive moves followed, climaxing in the fork that I spotted several moves prior. He hesitated, as he knew the game was all but lost. The game only lingered another few moves when he lost another piece and resigned the game.

I found myself sitting across from Mark Ryan, the state champion, at the head table for the sixth and final round. It was the classic underdog matchup, the two time state champ versus an inferior opponent coming from table thirteen. Everybody expected the champ to effortlessly stroll down victory lane, but they did not realize that the frustrations and effort in attempting to prevail over a physical assault by a random viral infection caused a twelve year old to develop his cranial capacity in pursuit of an area that he could triumphantly excel in. I knew that if I were to prevail, I'd have to play aggressively and leave nothing on the chess board. I was going to win big or lose bigger.

I played my usual opening where I worked defense and offense simultaneously. After all my pieces were developed, I launched an offensive that was blocked. This resulted in gridlock on the board and the game dragged on for another two hours. As we ran out of time on the clocks and as the number of pieces on the board slowly dwindled, I obtained a two pawn advantage. That was enough to give me the victory if I held on. He then checked me and I had only one place to move my king. He checked me again and I had to move it back. He did this six more times knowing that if the same pieces are moved back and forth six times, the result is a forced stalemate.

When the game was called, the waiting began. I was upset because I knew I had the game won, but now we had to wait while the officials determined whose opponents had the best record. As it turned out, my opponents had superior records, and I was the winner! My coach congratulated me saying, "You deserve it, you've been to hell and back the last few months and you didn't let that stop you!" I silently concurred and thought, "If anything, my physical condition propelled my need to succeed on the chess board." This was the first of many successive victories highlighting a distinguished ability to play chess.

Nutritional Triumph

Celebration of my recent victory was brief due to re-focusing on my rehabilitation effort and finding the ultimate solution to my mobility issues. The problem evolved from rubberized legs and incapacitation to a period of moderate muscular tone restoration through intense therapy then advanced to a point where the tightness and tone of my leg muscles produced an overcompensation of spasticity resulting in mild discomfort. I understood through discussions with the therapist weeks prior that my brain was constantly telling my muscles to contract to compensate for the muscle weakness left by the viral infection and lack of use.

I soon began noticing a startling catch-twenty-two; as my legs grew stronger through weight exercises, the spasms did not subside to allow the strength of my muscles to resume normal activity. However, the spasms increased in severity in proportion to my muscle development. This physiological paradox drove me, with the full support of my parents, to seek out any and every solution to find a mitigation of the disorder.

Thinking that the problem may have been triggered by dietary habits, we sought nutritional and holistic methods in finding a solution. We heard about a holistic doctor who was scheduled to host a seminar at our church, so my mother and I decided to ask his advice. After briefly summarizing the condition, he asked me to extend my left arm, and touch my thumb to my middle, index and little fingers. As I did this, he pushed down on my outstretched arm. He told me that there was a build-up of yeast in my body and he advised me to abstain from eating sugar and grains for two weeks. It was beyond me how the man made a determination of that sort by pressing my arm, but it seemed advantageous to follow his advice. Two weeks later, I still had the neuropathy but no headaches or upset stomach and I was less tired throughout the day. There were nutritional benefits in controlling sugar consumption. Even though the experiment did nothing to address the issue that I intended, it proved to be beneficial from a nutritional stance.

I was encouraged by our pursuit of a natural cure. My dad struck up a conversation with a nutrition guru one day when he went jogging at the park. Bob Duris came to our home to discuss his "latest and greatest" nutrition plan which he indicated to my dad "as beneficial for Ernie." The plan that he discussed with us was the "Master Cleanse" developed by Dr. Stanley Burroughs in the 1930s. Essentially, it's a mechanism of removing toxins from one's body that are picked up through poor dietary habits and through the environment, which are flushed out and eliminated through the Cleanse. Toxins are absorbed into the body through everyday living, causing people to develop illnesses that are preventable and potentially reversible if the agents that caused the symptoms are removed. Since my condition was caused by a viral infection, it seemed advantageous to drive it out through a deep tissue purification process which the "Master Cleanse" was designed to do.

The "Cleanse" was a simple concoction consisting of one cup of pure grade B maple syrup, four fresh squeezed lemons, one teaspoon of cayenne pepper mixed together in sixty ounces of purified water. We had to make a batch every morning and drink it throughout the day. I repeated this every day for ten days. The one catch was I must abstain from eating food for those ten days. The vitamins, minerals and enzymes within the maple syrup and lemon juice was sufficient to provide an adequate level of nutrients to sustain me throughout the process. The cayenne pepper served as the cleansing agent which would scour the internal organs as they rested from the normal digestive cycle. In mixing the ingredients in sixty ounces of water the elements were to be consumed equally throughout the day.

There were other things I had to do at the same time to enhance the cleansing process. I had to soak in hot peppermint water to facilitate perspiration thereby drawing toxins out through the skin. The skin is the largest body organ. I had to drink herbal laxative tea to maintain bowel movement and perform salt-water flushes.

These flushes consisted of a quart of sea-salt water that was consumed as quickly as possible. This swept through the digestive track within a half hour and carried all remaining debris on its way out. The first six days of this resulted in a clean colon, liver, skin and pancreas. The lungs, joints, and blood clean-out occurred during the latter portion. If an undesirable condition persists after ten days, a person extending the cleanse safely up to forty days may be advantageous.

During our dialogue with Bob, he offered testimonials where people were able to reverse advanced stages of cancer and other fatal diseases through this process and suggested that if the virus responsible for my neurological condition was still operating within my body, this was a way in prohibiting any further progression and reverse existing damage. The promise of anything ridding my body of the infection that was causing me so much grief was enough to convince me to try it, regardless of how extreme and insane it sounded. After all, I prided myself in being extreme and all out in everything I put my mind to. Nevertheless, a thirteen year old boy has to be desperate to forgo food for ten days, which I was.

I woke early to assist my mother in mixing the first batch. When I took the first sip, I almost vomited; it was worse than terrible. After the first glass, I didn't think it was possible to fast for ten days and drink something that tasted so horrible; going without food was more appealing than this. The second morning I woke up with severe hunger pains but these were alleviated as soon as I drank my 'lemonade'. From that point on, when I felt hungry I sipped on my drink. It suppressed the hunger pains through the consumption of nutrients and eliminated the psychological desire for food with the putrid smell, taste, and texture of the mixture.

My family and I were amazed. The benefits of the supplemental cleansing features of the program equally perplexed us. Each of us had similar timelines in experiencing extreme headaches and discomfort for the first three days due to the stirring up of toxins that were lodged in our bodies. The elimination of these toxins continued throughout the next seven days and we didn't fully realize the benefits of the ordeal until the completion of the cleanse. I immediately felt an increase in energy and stamina throughout daily activity. I no longer felt drowsy as I woke up. It was as if I had already drunk a pot of coffee.

My adrenalin level maintained its peak throughout the day. I found myself requiring less sleep as there were no toxins causing my body to require excess sleep. The most notable benefit proving the validity of the cleanse as a worthwhile component of nutritional wellness was the strengthening of my immune system to the point where I did not even develop a minor cold as long as I maintained a schedule of cleansing twice a year. This was crucial in that, since I fell sick a year earlier which resulted in a crippling condition, there had always been a psychological correlation between sickness and an inability to walk. If illnesses were preventable, aversion of regressing to my former condition was desirable. Having found a means of strengthening my immune system in prevention of sickness, it was advantageous to adopt this discipline and I continued to cleanse my body at least twice a year hence.

As I grew spiritually, I would incorporate prayer and study of the Bible which strengthened my spiritual immune system as well. It seemed appropriate that, as I was cleansing my physical body through the deprivation of foods that clogged the arteries and settled in the crevices of the colon and various other regions of the physical body, the same with my spiritual body was necessary. So during these cleansing periods, I would spend the hours that I normally spent eating and feeding my physical body with studies of the scripture and other supplemental books. During these days the consumption of food was replaced with the consumption of knowledge and wisdom from countless sources which proved helpful in addressing my personal, spiritual, and psychological battles; as well as assisting others in offering advice as during these times, God blessed me with wisdom well beyond my years.

The Mission Field

Another physical benefit attributable to the cleanse was observed while our family was privileged to act as servants of the Lord Jesus Christ via a short-term missions trip to Peru. As our airplane touched down in Cusco, Peru, located a few thousand feet above sea level, we were advised that we may become nauseous or sick due to the elevation until our bodies acclimated. My mother, father, and I experienced no such symptoms, however, my brother and sister, who failed to participate in the cleanse, experienced the symptoms.

Our purpose and mission in traveling to Peru was to help at an orphanage supported by a church pastored by a missionary whom we were acquainted with. The orphanage was situated outside Limatambu, a mountain village a two hour bus ride from Cusco. It was completely self-sufficient with the men building the adobe cottages in the same way Peruvians had for centuries. My dad and brother joined the natives in stacking the 70 pound adobe bricks to construct a dormitory. My mother, sister, and I helped harvest and shell the beans. We also cooked and dispersed large quantities of food in a church courtyard where many orphans assembled. Having the opportunity to participate in the fulfillment of the great commission was life-changing. I realized that my hardships were nominal when I witnessed true poverty and the disease and disabilities which were the result of harsh living conditions and lack of medical treatment. I had the privilege of knowing what awaits me at the end of my affliction, which many people, especially in developing regions, do not.

While we were in Peru, we had the opportunity to visit Macchu-Pichu, the ruins of an ancient Mayan city that was built on the side of a mountain. This decision was probably made for strategic reasons, however I thought at the time that the city became desolate after all the Indians fell off the mountain. It was another one of those "once in a lifetime experiences" according to my mother, so I had no option but to test fate by traversing hundreds of steep, narrow, jagged steps atop cliffs thousands of feet above the valleys. I don't know who had a rougher time, me or the local tour guide and tourists who audibly gasped in terror as they witnessed me time and time again stumble and fall inches away from the edge of a cliff.

An unassisted, visually impaired kid, years prior to my leg condition, hiking the Grand Canyon was enough to mortify people, but a nearly crippled blind kid, who's too fiercely independent to accept help from anybody, traversing perilous terrain was even more frightening. I recall on one such excursion to Hocking Hills, Mrs. Gage had to walk a sizable distance in front of me as she insisted that her heart would fail for fear if she remained back with my parents and me. I always completed these journeys with bruises, gashes, and lacerations. I kept my guardian angels busy with the responsibility to see that I lived another day.

Triumph of Strength

Throughout my early teen years, I continued my rehabilitation effort by lifting weights daily, walking on the treadmill, and the various other exercises I learned in therapy. I reached a point where I briefly laid my cane aside and walked unassisted, but soon regressed to utilizing my cane for balance. I never truly regained normal walking motion as understood by somebody with normal muscle development. It was more like a controlled falling forward. I allowed my body to fall forward, stick one leg out to catch me, and then let physics propel me forward in allowing my other leg to catch my body to repeat the motion. Despite the glass ceiling, where progression towards the goal of "normal walking" was prohibited, I exercised with as much intensity as if I was only one good workout away from full attainment of the prize.

The notion soon crossed my mind that if I lifted weights with my upper body, which wasn't affected by the neuropathy, and realize substantial muscle development, that satisfaction might diminish my frustrations at the stagnation I was experiencing with my legs. My time spent at the gym doubled. While my mother taught aerobics at the local YMCA, I worked out in the weight room intensely pumping iron.

I soon realized that the limitations governing the progress of my leg muscle development placed no such restrictions on my upper body. Like any 110 pound, thirteen year old, I started off pushing petty weights which paled in comparison to the heavy weights that I could hear clanging and thudding all around me. Through talking to people and by trial and error, I soon discovered what exercises to do and how many sets and repetitions to do for maximum muscle development. I began to set goals for myself, just as I did with my legs, but now instead of painstakingly pursuing a goal which was unattainable through a physiological abnormality, I set goals and surpassed them. After setting a goal of being able to pull, push, and press my body weight for ten repetitions within six months, I began setting far-reaching goals that I thought would be impossible to attain. Then I blasted past even those goals.

The biggest disadvantage about having the ability to lift heavier weight with my upper body was that in order to load the bar with weights, I had to carry 45 pound plates across the room. Normally I tripped over my toes while merely walking using a cane in my right hand to maintain balance. To transport the weights, I tossed my cane aside, grabbed onto the plate with both hands and began tripping across the weight room. I always thought to myself, "I hope nobody moved any furniture or left any weights in the middle of the floor for me to trip over." I relied on a mental mapping of the room layout to navigate about. On one of these trips, as the bar was almost fully loaded, I had the last 35 pound plate in my hands when I felt my toe catch on something. I knew I was about to crash. Instead of throwing the weight in my hands forward as I usually did to avoid dropping it on myself, I panicked and just let go of it. It fell straight down and landed squarely on my big toe. Pain shot up my leg which reminded me of another paradox of my condition. While my motor neurons were atrophying, my sensory neurons were hypersensitive amplifying faint touch as well as pain. Despite this, I had built up an incredible pain tolerance because it was a fact of life and unavoidable. So pressing through the pain, I finished my workout. Forty-five minutes later as I was taking off my shoes, I felt a warm, sticky substance that had seeped through. I quickly ripped of my shoe and peeled off my sock. I felt my toe and found it crushed and the toenail was gone. I thought it best to find my mom and ask her opinion. That led to a trip to the emergency room. An x-ray was taken at the hospital and since it was not broken they didn't do anything but clean it, put a little ointment on it, tape it to the toe next to it, send me on my way and charge my dad's insurance company a few hundred dollars. The very next day I was at the gym working out as if my foot wasn't throbbing.

Gym class had always posed problems for visually impaired students participating in the activities with a class of fully sighted counterparts. Now at Waite High School with limited sight and mobility the challenges escalated to where gym was dangerous if I was expected to fully engage in games and activities. I recalled how in junior high gym I was a sitting target in dodge ball because I couldn't see the ball. I was hit in the face many times by people whipping the ball at me and not realizing I couldn't see it. The same issue affected my ability to play basketball, volleyball, and baseball. Fortunately, the high school gym teacher, Carman Amenta, was my brother's wrestling coach and knew of my gym plight. He was aware of my dedication and passion for lifting weights, and he unlocked the weight room prior to the start of gym class and permitted me to spend the period with a student spotter doing what I enjoyed and what my body required.

I completed my leg exercises in solitude and returned at the end of the day to work my upper body with the wrestling team. It gave me a great deal of satisfaction when I, as a freshman, could keep up with the junior and senior athletes. My competitive nature was beginning to take over. I might not be able to play the sports that everybody else was successful at on account of my maladies, but it was quite an accomplishment for a "non-athlete" to be able to out-lift some of the best athletes in the school. To this end I would tirelessly push my body to the limits, spending hours in the gym each day. I was making gains so consistently that by the end of my sophomore year, I could bench press one and a half times my body weight twelve times in a row, do forty-five body dips without stopping and twenty-five chin-ups. It was not just I who recognized my uncanny ability to lift a tremendous amount of weight in proportion to my body weight. Soon different people began asking me if I had ever competed in weight lifting competitions. I never had, but this may be the outlet through which I could express my competitive nature in the physical arena and not solely demonstrations of cognitive superiority in chess competitions.

I brought up the idea of registering for a bench press competition with my mentor and friend Mr. Powell, who was the former Mr. Toledo Body Building Champion, to see what he thought. He too was very competitive by nature in every facet of life. However, I knew that he would be exceedingly excited if I followed in his footsteps in competitive weightlifting. I wasn't disappointed; he immediately started strategizing. He introduced me to Jimmy Mominee, the man who had trained him for the Mr. Toledo competition. Jimmy was a professional bodybuilder and also a record holder in three different weight classes for power lifting.

Jimmy instantly recognized the unusual drive, determination, and advanced strength that I had for a sixteen year old. We trained five days a week at the Powerhouse Gym in Toledo. We trained four months in preparation for the national bench press competition that was being held in Cleveland. It was a structured four month process where I had to master form and technique in order to be capable of handling the largest amount of weight possible. In addition to weight training, a proper diet of protein and carbohydrates was implemented.

As competition day approached, we discussed the set up of the meet. The night before the event every lifter was weighed. Then they had three opportunities to press the amount of weight of their choosing. Their highest weight was then divided by their recorded body weight. Whoever had the highest score won the competition. I was entered in the nineteen and under category, which meant competing against older kids. Any score above one and a half times their body weight is a decent score considering the age group. A week prior to the competition, Jimmy informed me that he was unable to attend, so Mr. Powel filled in as my spotter.

The night before the big day, after we arrived in Cleveland and went to weigh in, I was pleased to weigh in at 135 pounds exactly. It looked like my strict eating habits had paid off. The next morning we arrived to the venue early to scope out the competition. There were eighteen kids in the competition, most of whom were older than I. If I were to do well, I'd have to go all out and press more than what I'd ever pressed before.

We predetermined a moderate amount of weight to be the first attempt, something that could be handled easily just to lock in a decent score before attempting heavy weight. Mr. Powell asked the judges to have 235 pounds loaded on the bar. I drew the bar down and held it stable until the judges gave me the go ahead to press the weight. When they did, I quickly blasted the weight up with ease. I had the bar loaded with 275 pounds for my second attempt which was a weight that I'd barely pressed before in practice. The adrenaline surge from the competition made this remarkably easy. This weight shot up almost as fast as the first lift. As Mr. Powell and I approached the platform for the third and final lift my toe caught on the edge of the platform. I staggered around for a few moments to regain my balance and composure. My focus was broken and as I hurriedly lay on the bench, I struggled with the 290 pound barbell that guaranteed a first place finish. In the end I just didn't lock it out and gave up two inches away. I settled for fourth place with a score of 2.04.

I continued to compete in other bench press competitions as I continued to excel in upper body strength. One summer, I heard of a Christian evangelism team that was going to witness at a local church. The "Power Team" travels around the world and shares the gospel, utilizing the personal testimonies of the people on the team. The hook that they use in maintaining audience members attention is their incredible strength and athleticism. By braking bricks with all sorts of body parts, lifting heavy objects that have been set on fire, tearing telephone books in half and many other attention grabbing feats of strength, they were able to engage and maintain a captive audience.

I was enthralled in the various demonstrations as anything involving strength and muscle development amused me. Memories of the nights' performance occupied my thoughts, especially during my workouts, when I decided that some of the feats may just be the next challenge on my "to do" list. Projecting that there was a degree of technique involved in the feats, I sought out friends and acquaintances who were experts in related areas in teaching me how to appropriately focus my strength in performing the various feats.

I asked my friend Ralph, a proficient martial artist who was also one of my sparring chess opponents, to teach me the art of breaking bricks. He said, "Your lack of vision will help as most people focus on the surface of the top brick, driving through the bricks will be easier for you." Of course there were failed attempts, but I eventually grasped the physics involved and became proficient at breaking bricks with my hands, elbows and even head. The concept of focusing on the end result, rather than the obstacle was equally applicable to the other desired feats. In visualizing myself breaking an unopened can of soda like an egg, the tolerance level of the can is surpassed, ending in the desired result. I practiced my tearing technique by stacking magazines on top of each other, gradually reaching telephone book thickness, at which point the goal was reached. Other feats involving a greater degree of brute strength, such as rolling a frying pan up like a burrito and snapping the chain on handcuffs, were later added to my repertoire.

The insurmountable paradox frustrated me to no end; attainment of any goal I put my mind to relating to upper body muscular development while struggling just as hard with leg strengthening to only have the condition worsen. It did not make rational sense to me. Why did God allow an insatiable appetite for muscular development to be satisfied in my upper body, while permitting my lower extremities to self-destruct? I much preferred to make a transaction, if possible, to exchange all of my hard work and dedication involved in attaining a high level of upper body performance for lower body regularity.

87

Suffering Relapse and Implantation

I was as thrilled with my bench pressing competition and strength training as I had been with my victory several years earlier in a high ranking chess tournament. Yet, I was still dissatisfied with my recent success. The only satisfaction at this time was possible through complete restoration of my ability to walk and run uninhibited, which did not occur. I welcomed at least incremental steps and victories in my rehab efforts, something that gave me substantial hope that restoration one day was possible, but nothing was forthcoming. It was beyond me that my upper body strength developed the capacity to bench press more than double my body weight using incredible focus, dedication, determination, and perseverance, while no equivalent gains in my leg condition using these same techniques were realized. This was no psycho-symptomatic situation; the fallacy that overcoming the condition if I just worked hard enough was becoming more evident as time progressed. In fact, there seemed to be a regression. There was extreme tightening in my legs. This sent my family and me on another round of tedious, time-consuming doctor visits in search of solutions.

We decided not to go back to Dr. Sanders, the pediatric neurologist who saw me in the hospital. Visits to his office merely consisted of him walking in, doing tests of my vitals and reflexes and walking out muttering, "At least you're still walking." It was time to find somebody who was actually interested in finding the root of the problem. Another prominent pediatric neurologist in Toledo was a tall man known as the "Silent Giant." After observing me walk and the reflex tests, he suggested that I may have a form of cerebral palsy that was undetectable until early adolescence. He ordered a muscle biopsy, where he cut muscle tissue from my right leg while I was under anesthesia and sent it off to the lab for analysis. The results confirmed his thought; the muscular atrophy was not due to diseased muscle tissue, but rather solely a product of neuro-malfunction. He offered no additional advice because he was unable to identify why my neurons weren't functioning properly.

Alarmed at his suggestion of the condition being a severe, incurable condition and his inability to offer any further assistance, we traveled outside of Toledo to a well-respected pediatric neurologist in the state, Dr. Cameron. We waited in the reception room for two hours. I finally met the doctor. He performed the classic reflex test that I expected with every visit and he promptly scheduled an EMG test. Electrical Magnetic Graph is a test where needles connected to wires are inserted directly into the muscles. These send a series of signals to a computer which graphs the muscle activity on a computer monitor. I knew the drill. I had been subjected to this uncomfortable test while I was in the hospital, and tried with all my will power to move my legs and feet in response to the doctor's commands to generate the highest reading possible on the monitor. A few minutes passed during which he asked me repeatedly if I was trying to move. Of course I had been giving my utmost effort. He finally put the instruments down and said "It's a miracle that you are even able to walk at all!" This response was not surprising to me. I was conscious that my mental fortitude was great enough to attain things that were physically impossible; a fortitude which was divinely placed inside of me by the One who knew I needed the trait to overcome the mountains in my life.

During the consultation with my mother and I, the doctor

explained that the classification of disorder that I was experiencing was known as spastic paraplegic neuropathy; which essentially means that there was a neurological disorder causing my legs to become very tight. He went on to explain that the spasms produced by my brain was a means of artificially causing my leg muscles to be strengthened enough to carry my body weight. One of the unfortunate consequences of the extreme spasticity was that the larger muscles naturally overpowered the antagonistic muscle thereby accelerating the remission of the smaller muscle groups. My calf muscle eventually rendered my anterior tibialis useless and my quadriceps did the same to my hamstrings. We had already seen evidence of this because I was perpetually tripping over my toe.

Before he prescribed a series of major drugs to treat the symptoms, Dr. Cameron referred me for another stint of extreme therapy at the therapy wing of the YMCA in Perrysburg, Ohio. These sessions were identical to the sessions I endured years before and maintained throughout the years on my own initiative. The only major difference was acute focus on strengthening the minor muscle groups to offer them an opportunity to contend with the major muscle groups. The therapist periodically measured the dexterity on my legs, ankles and toes. We found that my toes were already completely paralyzed, so no therapy was in order there. My ankles had thirteen percent movement when compared with normal ankle motion and the legs had sixty-five percent dexterity. Realizing the full severity of the problem I was up against, I applied myself to pursue the full recovery of my members with a ferocity that I hadn't unleashed until that point. By this time I understood the neuroplastic nature of the brain, which God in His wisdom had instilled there. The brain is compiled of one hundred trillion neurons, each with seventy-thousand dendrites with the capacity to reconfigure themselves to regain lost activity. I had read that people utilized this concept in retraining their brain after severe spinal cord injuries, brain biopsies or amputations in ridding themselves of phantom pain. With this hope, I worked out maintaining mental imagery of myself performing the individual functions as if I had nothing inhibiting my performance -- to no avail.

After a few months of progressively stronger spasms, Dr. Cameron prescribed oral Baclofen. Baclofen is a very potent neurotoxin which, amongst other things, blocks the excretion of gabanine, a chemical excreted through the spinal column that controls muscle spasticity. My body was releasing too much gabanine to my leg muscles, and by blocking it, there was a reduction in the spasms. Severe liver and kidney damage was a danger if too much oral baclofen was ingested. For this reason blood was drawn every six weeks for analysis to determine if the levels in my blood were dangerously elevated. I underwent an eight week trial of the oral form of medication. There was a moderate decrease in my spasms as my dosage was increased. This was the first promising treatment of my symptoms that was encountered.

After I indicated that the oral baclofen was minimally effective and I might receive more benefit if the dosage was increased, Dr. Cameron explained that the medication was at the highest permissible dosage without complications with poisoning the internal organs and potential cognitive consequences. He went on to suggest that I was a prime candidate for a drug infusion system, which was an internal pump that administered a very small fraction of the drug directly to the spinal cord via a catheter; thus transcending the blood barrier. This allowed me to receive an adequate dose of this medication without danger of liver toxicity, so I agreed to try it out.

On the day of the trial, Dr. Cameron instructed me to lie on my side, curl up in a fetal position, keep my arms around my knees and squeeze as tight as possible. He jabbed a needle into my spinal cord. While painful, this sensation no longer shocked me, and he released five hundred micrograms, equivalent to one day's dose of the medication, in the course of six seconds. Within a minute, I had the most euphoric sensation come over me; my legs were completely loose. I did not remember the day that my legs were unencumbered by uncomfortable and painful contractions. I was instantly hooked, it didn't matter what the catch was. I was 17 and being offered relief from five years of physical anguish. I found out as soon as I attempted to stand to go to the restroom what the drawback was. I sat on the edge of the bed unsure if I was to trust my legs. I transferred my full body weight from the bed to my legs and as I did I hit the ground just the way I had when I fell sick five years prior. I contemplated this new dilemma. It was the spasticity which was keeping my legs strong enough to walk. As soon as it was taken away, so was my ability to walk.

The surgery to implant the pump was scheduled for early June after my junior year in high school. Dr. Geiger was the surgeon, a pediatric neurosurgeon who had implanted about a dozen pumps. He met with my parents and me to advise us of what to expect during the surgery and the recovery process. There was approximately a six to eight day in-patient recovery to allow the spinal cord to heal around the freshly inserted catheter.

I underwent the surgery and when I woke up, I didn't have any pain. I was determined to abbreviate my stay at the hospital. I was lying flat on my back with no pillow under my head so my spinal cord fluid didn't leak. That can cause extreme headaches. I was already too familiar with those and not eager to have one.

Gradually the effects of the anesthesia dissipated and the four inch incision in the lower left side of my stomach began to throb. In addition to that, the hockey puck-sized pump that was now in me began to sting. All of this was combined with aching where the catheter entered my spinal cord. This latter sensation was the most bothersome because it was a new kind of pain.

Despite increasing severity in pain as the healing process took its course, I correlated pain medication with "wimpiness" and refused to take any. Next to the psychological struggle of being flat on my back, confined to a hospital bed for six days, the most excruciating part of the ordeal was swallowing my ego when I needed to void. I couldn't hold it after the second day. Initially I had planned to be able to hold it until I was mobile to make it to the commode, but no such providence. Upon submitting my request for the appropriate device I thought, "This is where the nurses make their money!"

After four days on my back completely, without so much as raising my head, I attempted to sit up. Pain shot up in my head and forced me to the mattress for two more days. On the seventh day I was determined to not only sit up, but to walk out of the hospital regardless how badly my head was pounding. I did just that. The nurse asked if I had any pain. I knew if I said yes two more days was imminent in the hospital so I told them I didn't.

The new unit was working well, although the level of

looseness was not the same as in the trial because the doctor had the mechanism set to release ninety micrograms throughout the course of a day. My legs were noticeably more relaxed than a week earlier when I was just taking the oral Baclofen. After a few days of walking about, however, the tightness started slowly creeping back into my legs. I now possessed the power to combat this spasticity by increasing the dosage that the pump released, so I went to visit Cheri Lee who was charged with maintaining my pump. I requested an increase and she upped the dose ten percent. A few days later I felt my muscles relax but a few days after that they were beginning to tighten up again. I promptly took the bus over to St. Vincent's Hospital to have Cheri increase the medication another ten percent. This cycle perpetuated itself until I was receiving four-hundred and forty-two micrograms of Baclofen a day and I realized I was chasing after that complete relaxation sensation just like a druggie pursues another snort of cocaine. Just like a druggie I'd never attain the first release I'd experienced. Realizing this was my plight, I resolved to maintain a constant level and merely visit Cheri for refills of the device twice a year.

The spasms eventually progressed to the severity they were prior to my Baclofen treatment. My experiential conclusion was that the spasms, destructive as they were, were my brain's way of artificially reinforcing my leg strength so my ability to walk was quazi-maintained. Any attempt to reduce or eliminate spasticity was met with an increase in spasticity.

I was back to square one in accepting the spasms as a fact of life and I faced the need to cope with them rather than eliminating them. Aerobic exercise soon took on a two-pronged purpose: not only was it necessary to facilitate blood flow and nimbleness, but I gleaned psychological benefits as well. I physically exhausted my body throughout the course of a day to force my body to fall asleep at night. This assisted in preventing me from tossing and turning from the spasms. The exercising also alleviated depressing emotions resulting from my condition. Furthermore, mental exhaustion kept my hyperactive mind tired so I wasn't up until four or five in the morning. I did this by using my adaptive equipment to consume book after book of any topic imaginable at breakneck speed. On average, I would listen to and fully comprehend five to seven full length books a week in addition to my academic and Bible studies. This passion was not feasible outside of having a debilitating neuropathy as a driving motivating factor.

A Gift of Sight

Ever since I was a little boy, I was embarrassed at having to parade around tapping a white stick with a red tip. I desired a cooler indicator of my vision loss. I always wanted a guide dog. As I was nearing adulthood I was also reaching an age where attainment of a guide dog was permissible. I didn't think a public high school was a conducive environment for a service animal, so I decided to bypass my senior year and enroll in college. In achieving this I used the post-secondary option, which is a program that allows academically eligible high school students to enroll either full or part time in a state funded university. I took the ACT and received a sufficient score to be admitted to the University of Toledo. My grade point average was also high enough to allow me to take a full class load at UT rather than attending Waite High School the following year.

After the plans for my final high school year were in motion, I began the process of finding the right guide dog school. There were thirteen schools across the nation that had different rules and regulations to obtain a dog. Schools differed in things like breeds of dogs utilized and whether someone could keep the dog after retirement. I opted to contact Pilot Dogs, Incorporated for three simple reasons: they allowed the recipient to keep the dog after retirement, they utilized seven different breeds of dogs -- one of which was boxers -- that I found intriguing, and the location of the school in Columbus, Ohio, which is approximately two hours from Toledo. I submitted the application including an eye doctor's recommendation, personal references, and my first, second, and third preference of dog breed. I anxiously waited for acceptance. Much to my delight, I received a letter stating that a class beginning in the month of June had an opening, which was perfect timing as I had no conflicting obligations.

Pilot Dogs Incorporated is a non-profit organization whose mission is to equip visually impaired and blind individuals with guide dogs. They are primarily funded through the Lions Club, a foundation started by Helen Keller. At the time I attended the school, Pilot Dogs Inc. trained one hundred fifty teams a year. The operating expenses of the facilities, staff salaries, room and board for recipients and the various other expenditures necessary to run such an agency divided by the number of dogs trained was equivalent to about ten thousand dollars per dog. Because the expense was so great, the organization offers the liberating services of a fully trained guide dog to a recipient free of charge.

The process entailed traveling to Columbus and living in an onsite dormitory for a month with twelve other individuals in the class.   The first three days was spent walking around with the trainer; she gauged our stature, pace, gait, and other factors in determining the most appropriate match.   After this period, Pam, the trainer, selected a dog from the pool of trained dogs that she felt confident of working well with the recipient. Pam matched me with a fifty-pound, two-year-old brindle boxer named Calypso. We bonded instantly due to the rigorous four month regiment that the dogs are subject to during the isolated training program where the only human interaction they are exposed to is with the trainers. Needless to say after doggy boot camp, they are more than ready to come out of the kennel and be matched with a person.

The next three and a half weeks were spent walking around the compound, throughout neighborhoods, downtown, in rural areas and inside buildings with our dogs. We were exposed to every kind of traffic situation and environment so that we were prepared to independently navigate any area with our dogs.   It didn't take me long to see why I was matched with Calypso. Besides being my first choice in breed, I needed a dog that was small and agile enough to avoid being crushed by an unexpected crash, yet stocky enough to absorb an impact when the inevitable happens.

Calypso and I were an instant match and she was my right-hand dog. She quickly surpassed me in popularity. Any time I ventured out without my sidekick, people asked, "Where's Calypso?" before the typical salutations.   Calypso's permanent assignment led her on adventures that guide dogs only dream about.   From the moment we met we spent ninety-nine percent of our time together. She accompanied me through seven years of college classes, attending every lecture that I endured.   She traveled to the busy metropolitan area of Washington D.C., where she was trounced about in the subway with hundreds of hurried people failing to notice a twenty-two-inch dog. She kept pace throughout the streets of Toledo, busily campaigning with her charm as I ran for city council. She faithfully led without complaining through all climatic conditions: freezing cold, scorching heat, and torrential rain.

Academic Triumph

My joint senior year in high school/ freshman year in college climaxed with the AERO Award (Association for Education and Rehabilitation of the Blind and Visually Impaired of Ohio) for exemplary academic performance. The award was granted to two visually impaired or blind high school students within the state of Ohio who successfully demonstrated superior academic performance. Hope Rader, the assigned visually impaired instructor from Toledo Public Schools, had nominated me based on the work which she oversaw during her tenure as my instructor. The initiative demonstrated in becoming fully independent through utilization of my adaptive software programs, rather than using a person, was the primary reason for my nomination. Supporting factors included my grade point average throughout high school, stellar performance on state aptitude tests and outstanding study habits which culminated in early enrollment in college. The ceremony was held at the Deer Creek Resort, where a delightful dinner was served in a luxurious environment. After dinner, I delivered a stirring speech detailing the hardships visually impaired students faced throughout their educational experience and how overcoming them can be possible through the proper assistance.

A vindicating experience occurred in my last year of high school during the mandatory Multi-factor Evaluation that I was subject to every three years. I held fond memories of these tests and it never ceased to amaze my parents and me of the discontinuity between common sense and knowledge that these highly educated psychologists demonstrated. It is as if they did not read the notes on the existing condition of the pupil they were to test prior to that student walking in the room. Even when the conditions were brought to their attention, they continued utilizing the same script of a visual IQ test and consider the results as valid despite the subject being visually impaired! Finally a supervisor realized their error and decided to give me an auditory IQ test. In keeping with the uncommon sense prevalent in the Toledo Public Schools, this auditory IQ test was proctored by a PhD from Africa who had a very thick accent.

Dr. Mosidi read questions, trying hard to enunciate, and I issued an answer. One of the sections entailed him reading a sentence that I had to repeat verbatim from memory. After that, he'd read two sentences which I repeated in the same manner. This pattern would continue until I was repeating paragraphs. I had to make mental assertions of some of the content because I didn't understand Dr. Mosidi's thick accent. Eventually I grew frustrated at the tedium of the test and requested that the test be over. He honored my request, which meant he then had to score an incomplete test. A few days later, as several faculty members, my mother, Dr. Mosidi, and I were attending the IEP meeting, he confidently revealed the results of the test showing that I scored above the ninety-sixth percentile on all sections except one -- the incomplete test while transcending the language barrier!

Chapter 6

College?

      I have been confident of the direction of my career path ever since I was fifteen-years-old. I was touched by the Holy Spirit and had an overwhelming sense of purpose and destiny. From that moment, I knew everything that I put my mind to, provided I consecrated it to the Lord, was to be blessed. With that revelation I sought after a career path for God to utilize me to execute a portion of His divine plan. I did not fully understand that a direction God places in somebody's heart is subject to change at junctures unforeseen. I felt that the direction of my calling was in the legal profession. Through my extensive study of the foundation of the United States of America, there was an evident, direct relationship between prosperity of the nation and degree of adherence to biblical principles by the majority of citizens and public officials. The tipping point marking departure of the United States from Biblical principle and subsequently a forfeiture of blessings occurred with the secularization of the judicial process.

Reforming back to a God fearing society by combating the innate, atheistic judicial activism that has gripped America's once God-fearing legal institutions entails people with a conviction of the necessity of returning to the God of our forefathers. Joining the ranks of the devoted contemporaries, such as Jay Seculo with the American Center for Law and Justice entailed tutelage in the art of litigation at an accredited law school. The first step to that end was attainment of a Bachelor's degree. Attorney friends advised me to study a field that I enjoyed as it did not matter what my undergraduate degree was in. This led me to select political science as my preferred field of study because of my interest in the history of politics and the political nature governing the legal realm.

Confident in my degree choice, I selected a course schedule for my first year in college that satisfied the elective requirements for the college. Prior to the start of classes, my parents and I went to the University of Toledo to orient me with the layout of the campus in determining where my particular classes were located, and also to register with the Office of Accessibility, which is responsible for testing accommodations provisions and also to facilitate note-taking for students who can't see the visual lecture notes of the professor. As with prior unfamiliar geographies where my mental conceptualization of directions quickly created mental maps, it allowed me to memorize the entire campus, buildings included, within a matter of days. However, if this internal global positioning system was ever disrupted, my sidekick Calypso was there to steer me back on track. It wasn't long before she developed a habit of slightly deviating from a direct route to a destination on extremely hot or cold days, walking through a building that otherwise wasn't on the route to cool down or to warm up, a practice that I didn't mind as she always delivered me to my destination on time.

My normal waking rituals consisted of performing power-stretches. Stretches where I would grab my foot, rest my forearm on my shin, and in a hyper-extended position, pull unmercifully in order to stretch my hamstring. I performed similar contortions focusing on various muscles to make walking bearable while I listened to my joints and tendons groan under the pressure as if to say, "If you keep this up, we may give way." I was always in a hurry, wolfing down breakfast and shoving off for the closest bus stop. The bus arrived within a window of twenty minutes, fluctuating daily, unknown to the rider, so it was either be at the stop prior to the earliest arrival time or risk missing the bus completely. The bus then traveled around the entire East Side to the furthest possible bridge from downtown, and when on the other side of the river, back track to the bus loop which was literally one mile from my parents house by way of the closest bridge. This extended what was a five minute bus ride to twenty. I then waited fifteen minutes for another bus downtown to take me to the university. The connecting bus ride to the university was a jerky stop and go ride, with the driver smashing on the brakes to stop for passengers every quarter-mile or so. The rides home entailed a reverse pattern of the previously mentioned trip. It was not unusual for coach drivers to pass me up; I questioned them about the passover the next time I rode and they responded with the excuse, "I didn't see you," which was a valid excuse had I been driving. This caused the ten mile journey from my house to the university to exceed two hours on several occasions.

Needless to say, the endless traveling detracted from my study time, and waiting outside on a busy street exposed to the elements, constantly being splashed with muddy water by careless drivers, grew tiresome in a hurry. A remedy for this situation came with a decision to move into the Academic House on campus for my sophomore and junior years. This permitted me to focus on much needed studying as well as allowing me to participate in campus activities which had been previously unavailable due to my devotion of the majority of my non-class and study time in traveling to and from school.

The "Voice of Reason"

Arriving on time to class was possible by living on campus. I utilized the recreation center in continuation of my intense combination of rehabilitation and stress-relief program, attending the sporting events and extracurricular activities that I desired was possible, and I still had ample time for studying to achieve my goal of being on the dean's list. One activity that I soon found myself engaging in was broadcasting on the university's radio station. I was introduced to the group by an elementary school friend who had a show where he would broadcast Blues music. I was interested in the concept, not because I wanted to spin records, but because I wanted to try something unique. I wanted to try airing my opinions on the radio as I enjoyed listening to the local and national commentaries of the news by the popular pundits.

When I was fully trained on the radio equipment, having to memorize the various boards, decks, and displays by touch, I selected a slot from 6:00 AM to 8:00 AM to broadcast. I called my show "The Voice of Reason" because as with most other conservative commentators, my way of thinking and analyzing the news was steeped in common sense. One feature which separated my style from most of the mainstream syndicated opiners was that I didn't belittle the alternative viewpoints. Focusing on the conservative approach superseded the need to belittle opinions which did not identify with my own. This optimistic attribute, blended with confidence and charisma made for an entertaining and popular college talk show.

On my talk show days, I rose at 4:30 AM, rolled out of bed and staggered up the hill from my dorm room to the campus police station to retrieve the key for the radio station (as there was not anybody to open the station for me) at the Student Union in time for my show. After I made the quarter-mile, uphill trek to the police station, I had the same distance on a downhill grade. On the way I rehearsed the content of upcoming conversations. This early morning workout got the blood flowing, adrenaline pumping, and perspiration dripping so when I waltzed into the station, I was fully alert for another exciting show. I scrambled to push in the disk containing my opening songs and bumper music. After the first monologue, lasting the first fifteen minutes, I played a string of patriotic songs allowing me to get my first guest on the line who had agreed to come on the radio in the prior days. Guests consisting of professors, staff and faculty members of the university, local politicians and whoever agreed to come on the show with their relevant issues to the mission were welcome. Two guests were interviewed on each show with listeners calling in to ask them questions when I opened the line. The remainder of the show was comprised of commentary on local and national issues. There was no true way to gauge the listening audience, although I did receive calls on occasion from people who had been listening to the show from out of state. I never had dead air time on account of the steady stream of callers when the line was open.

Working in Washington D.C.

My undergraduate advisor, Dr. Lindeen, during one counseling session advised me of an internship opportunity that was available for all political science students to work for an agency in Washington D.C. to gain experience in a field of interest. This was an opportunity that I desired to take advantage of despite the steep monetary commitment in addition to the University of Toledo tuition. To defray these additional expenditures, I applied for and received scholarships requiring academic essays, which mitigated the costs, thereby making it possible for me to participate in the experience. I opted to attend The Washington Center, which is a liaison organization between universities worldwide and the agencies within Washington D.C. that accepted interns.

At the time of my application, there were several openings in the United States Attorney's Office, which I was strongly interested in because of my future ambition for law school. I heard two weeks prior to departure for the capital that I was selected for a position in my desired agency and expectantly anticipated a positive experience in working in my future occupation. A week later my parents, my sister, and I loaded the car and traveled to Virginia to stay with my dad's cousin, who lived in a suburb of DC, to provide orientation to the metro system as well as the layout of the metropolitan area.

Each day we drove to the closest subway terminal located in Springfield, Virginia and rode the Blue Line into the Capital. I have never experienced such a well organized, efficient public transit system; a far cry from TARTA that was so grossly inefficient. Six subway lines branched out like spokes to the suburbs in Virginia on the south and Maryland to the north. The different lines intersected at different strategic transfer locations, where passengers transferred to another line, or the opposite direction on the same line, exit the terminal to walk to their destination or board a bus which was coordinated with the subway to form one of the most efficient metropolitan transit systems in the world. Terminals, trains, and buses were equipped with automated systems identifying the current location, route, direction, and final destinations, which also made it the most accessible system I've ever traveled. In fact, I became so familiar with the system that I provided detailed directions to my roommates and others within two weeks of using the system.

We visited The Washington Center's headquarters, just down the street from the Foggy Bottom metro stop and met all the staff members. In addition to my internship obligations, I was scheduled to take a National Security class which met every Tuesday night. After a few more days of sightseeing with my parents and identification of guiding landmarks in order to navigate the city, I checked into my apartment located in a twelve level complex in Arlington, Virginia, immediately across the Potomac River from the Capital. The complex was situated a quarter mile from a metro stop and was equipped with a workout facility, drycleaners, and convenience store, as well as having grocery stores and a farmers' market in close proximity to the building.

The interns enrolled in the program were expected to be at their assigned location promptly at the beginning of the next work day. Being assigned to a division within the U.S. Attorney's Office, I was to arrive at a building located at the Judiciary Triangle metro-stop at 9:00 AM. I eagerly hopped out of bed at 6:00, performed my rituals, ate breakfast, put on my suit and walked down the street to the Courthouse stop which was located on the Orange Line - the same line as Judiciary Triangle. Two stops passed and the loudspeaker announced, "Now approaching Judiciary Triangle." I knew we traveled under the river, and a few miles into the Capital, but I never knew that public transit was capable of traveling so swiftly; such a difference between what I was used to and what I experienced in Washington. Contrary to common belief, the larger and more densely populated a metropolitan area is, the more conducive it is for visually impaired and blind people to travel due to the increased adherence to the Americans with Disabilities Act Guidelines that the administration of the system can fulfill due to more sustainable funding.

Upon arrival at my assigned building, I was sent to report to the fifth floor, which I soon discovered was the Superior Court, Criminal Division for the District of Columbia. Usually those types of court proceedings are handled by state governments, but since there is no state jurisdiction governing Washington DC, the federal government is responsible for prosecuting felony charges. I was enthusiastic to receive such an assignment, as criminal prosecution law was one of the fields that I desired to practice after graduation from law school. This experience allowed me to determine if it was worthwhile or if I was selecting a career path of endless boredom, tedium, and chronic exasperation as I had observed in most other litigious professions.

The first day was spent familiarizing myself with the floor, meeting the dozen attorneys who I was working for and submitting my software programs to the Information Technology department so the computer was usable in the office I was assigned. It wasn't long before somebody knocked on my door and asked me to make copies for them. I eagerly jumped to my feet, grabbed the files, and made my way over to the copier. I opened the lid and proceeded to place every piece of paper on the glass, aligned as best as possible with the raised ridges on the side of the copier. The copies must not have turned out as anticipated as I was never asked to make copies again. Word quickly spread throughout the office, "Don't have the blind intern make copies!" After the failed photocopy attempt, an attorney, Leah Bellere, had me attend court with her, attend depositions, talk to witnesses, and prepare briefs, allowing me to engage in all the activities in bringing a case to trial. Prior to cases being assigned, evidence must be sufficient for a grand jury to indict the defendant. After the case was assigned and all the evidence and witnesses were assembled, it seemed that the threshold of "beyond a reasonable doubt" was surpassed by a sizable margin in many of the cases that I assisted with and observed. Even still, it never ceased to amaze me of the proportion of juries, despite the preponderance of evidence, who returned a case with "not guilty" verdicts. I observed firsthand a case in which an eyewitness, as well as a surveillance camera, positively identified a defendant as being the assailant to a homicide, and despite the murder weapon, circumstantial, and DNA evidence pointing to the defendant, a jury found the defendant "not guilty!" There was no other plausible explanation other than the OJ effect, which turned out to be more prevalent than I anticipated. I pondered as to why anybody spent hours upon hours preparing a case, only to present it to a group of people with the preconceived notion of innocence. Even if this anomaly only occurs in a small percentage of the overall cases, it was too much for me and I began questioning whether I could tolerate devoting a career in the pursuit of justice in a system where the deck is stacked against prosecutors and victims.

One of my favorite leisure activities while in Washington was playing chess at Dupont Circle after work or on the weekends. I recalled watching a movie entitled "Searching for Bobby Fisher," where dozens of die-hard chess fanatics, from all walks of life played chess indiscriminately with one another in Central Park, New York. This was a similar environment where homeless people played each other and professionals, either to exercise strategic thought superiority, monetary gain, or both.

John, a fellow I met on my way to lunch one afternoon who was living in a halfway house, introduced me to the chess hot spot. I quickly noted the many contributing factors responsible for this mass assembly, in addition to a love for the game. Many of the individuals were homeless and chess was their only means of revenue. My principle in abstention from gambling benefited me greatly, as my odds of winning in Vegas may have been higher. I was accustomed to the oral bantering accompanying any lively chess match, as I grew up playing at the pawn shop in downtown Toledo where the art of jive talk was perfected.

Meanwhile, the class that I was taking with Dr. Henderson

was going well. He advised us on the first day that the structure and content of the class was equivalent to a graduate level course. This meant there was a heavy reading load, which I had no problem with, seminar discussions, where "The Voice of Reason" had prepared me well for oration, and an extensive research paper, which was not a problem due to my exceptional ability to process large volumes of information. The class also had the opportunity to assist him in hosting a fellowship conference for researchers that traveled from around the nation to meet in Washington D.C. for the annual Fellowship Forum for the Center for the Study of the Presidency, of which Rob Henderson was the President.

There was a fair amount of walking involved in traveling during my stay in the Capital. I walked the quarter-mile jaunt back and forth from my apartment and the metro at least once a day. I then trekked from the Judiciary Triangle metro-stop to my office building and goferred back and forth to the court house multiple times a day. Another one-way mile walk was necessary to travel from Foggy Bottom to The Washington Center's headquarters for class and other meetings. It was necessary to walk at least three miles a day in uncomfortable dress shoes that did not conform to my feet. By this time, the unrelenting contractions by the major muscle groups in my feet and ankles had left my feet with arches as steep as the Arch of St. Louis. Special fiber-glass casts were manufactured months prior by an orthotics specialist, which were to be worn at night in an attempt to correct this problem. The only problem was that the convulsions were so acute, that within a few nights of use, the casts were shattered.

Coping rather than correction became the goal. So to ease the discomfort, high-top tennis shoes were worn on all occasions.

However, tennis shoes weren't the appropriate attire for a young professional, so I decided to concede comfort for dress protocol and sported the latest high-heel Georgios. Two and a half months of walking around in these shoes led to the big toe on my left foot developing a sharp pain which grew stronger the more I walked on it. One evening as I was massaging it to ease the discomfort I felt my fingers slip as if to run over the toe, yet the skin was still beneath my fingertips. A few more strokes and I realized in shock what was happening; the skin on the bottom of my toe fell off! I quickly went over to the medicine cabinet where I always kept a large supply of antiseptic cream and a large box of Band-Aids. I rubbed some cream on the exposed meat of my toe, held the detached skin firmly in place where it ought to have been and taped it firmly in place with the Band-Aids. I hoped that this make-shift operation would cause the regenerative qualities of the body to heal around the skin that I carefully put back in place. I walked around for a few days in this condition, performing my maintenance procedure every night and finally realized the piece of skin I was tending was decaying.

At this point the shooting pain, every time I took a step, mandated that I have the condition checked out by a medical professional. Subsequently, I made an appointment with a podiatrist at George Washington University Hospital who informed me that I had developed an ulcer that had made its way to the bone. As she cut away the remainder of the dead skin, wrapped the toe very well in a bandage and wrote a prescription, she wondered aloud how it was possible for me to tolerate the pain until it digressed to such a point prior to seeking medical treatment. I responded by informing her of my neurological condition that inherently left a perpetual Charley-horse sensation in my legs that necessarily caused a mental blockage of the pain, which unfortunately caused "good" pain to be ignored as well. Fortunately, the prescription took effect quickly and the toe was back to normal within a few months; thus amputation was avoided.

As the time of my internship drew to a close, I assessed all of my experiences in deducing which path to take upon graduation. Law school was less appealing due to my recent experience and not to mention law schools across the nation were virtual machines cranking out lawyers, thereby over-saturating the field. Although I didn't rule this possibility out completely at this time, I considered other options. Rob Henderson, my instructor and President of the CSP, extended a fellowship opportunity to me to become a researcher at his think-tank. Although this was an appealing proposition, I wasn't prepared to move for an extended period of time away from friends and family back in Toledo. Other factors, such as cost of living, travel expenses, etc. factored in the decision to bypass this wonderful opportunity to secure gainful employment. Even still, I needed compelling justification to go back to Toledo, and it came in an attempt to contribute to society in the city I was born. As I thought about this, I devised a plan to utilize my skills, talents, and abilities in civil servitude in running for a political office upon graduation. I knew that city council elections were coming up in the upcoming fall; I could run for a district seat, thereby satisfying my need to keep busy in contributing to the forward progress of the city of my birth.

Out Standing in the Rain?

Upon arrival back in Toledo, I enlisted in my final round of classes. Graduate school of some sort would certainly be around the corner. But for now it was time to conclude my first four years of higher education and hang the diploma on my wall. The semester started well and I was preparing for a strong finish to catapult me into the real world. The hundreds of dollars spent on books and the countless miscellaneous charges which nickel and dime the college student to death and now the graduation fees were coming in to shake every last penny out of my already empty pockets. For this reason, I eventually stopped opening the mail that I received from the University of Toledo. I feared yet another letter with another made up charge designed for the University to reach into my "open checking account."

One afternoon, my mother informed me that there had been an envelope addressed from the Department of Arts and Sciences setting on the table for the last two weeks. I told her that I had no interest in opening it, but she may open it if she wanted; "Just pay the bill as well!" Upon opening the envelope, she exclaimed, "You were selected to receive the Deans Award for Outstanding Student in the Department of Political Science and Public Administration!" I was flattered of course, but was hesitant to accept the award as there was probably a registration fee for the reception, in which case I would pass up the honors.

Upon attending the ceremony, it was discovered that the Deans Award was a high honor bestowed on one graduating senior from each department in the College of Arts and Sciences for outstanding academic performance and degree of scholastic performance throughout the previous four years. Criteria such as grade point average, quality of research, and general consensus amongst the departmental faculty were taken into consideration in selecting the candidate. I was privileged, of course, to receive recognition for academic excellence at the college level to accompany my prior awards in academics and other areas. But I knew that supportive factors in attaining such honors were an ambition spawned out of circumstances that if otherwise not exposed to, the motivation in achieving such things were less likely. This attribute tempered with an identity and confidence in Christ Jesus instilled within me the ability to transcend all obstacles in perseverance. For simplicity purposes, when people asked me what the Outstanding Student Award was, I replied, "It most likely had to do with all the sightings of me out standing in the rain, waiting for the bus!"

Chapter 7

The Campaign

    I announced at my college graduation party, with my family and close friends in attendance, my intention to run for City Council. Understanding that Toledo City Council was comprised of both At-Large and District councilman, I anticipated taking out a petition for the East Side district where I reside. This limited the campaign to fifty-thousand residents. When I met with an official at the Lucas County Board of Elections, I was informed that the only elections being held that year were the Mayoral and At-Large contests. Without skipping a beat, I asked for the At-Large petitions, thinking that a citywide campaign was only slightly larger.

    The first order of business was securing two thousand

signatures on the official petitions from eligible registered voters to have my name printed on the primary ballots, a task I thought would be relatively easy to achieve. I was familiar with petition drives and went to the first mass assembly of people that was scheduled for the year to start soliciting signatures - the Sacred Heart Festival. I enthusiastically summarized the essentials of a solid government with individuals prior to asking them for their vote. I pitched my line to Carty Finkbeiner, the former Mayor of Toledo; he proceeded to invite me to a meeting that he was hosting the following morning at the Teamsters Hall and asked me to be prepared to give a speech.

That night I pondered what I would say the next morning and delivered a passionate speech that received a standing ovation. The content of the speech was not that different than the average local politician. However, the passion and charisma that I delivered it with was enough to get people stirred up. I realized then and there, as long as one can keep an even keel on controversial issues and stay simple, elections were nothing more than popularity contests.

Knowing full well the historical importance of an informed and engaged electorate, I understood the reality of twenty-first century politics filled with politically correct rhetoric and empty promises. I resolved to run a campaign free of that and instead revert back to the foundational ideology incumbent on a statesman with good moral character, although my core belief was that breaking the chains off Toledo would involve leadership of good moral character, sound judgment, and the fear of God. I quickly found out that this doctrine was no longer welcomed by the public, so abstention from talking about the core issues was conducive for

117

a successful campaign in the City of Toledo. I remembered well when my mother ran for Toledo Public School Board; she was lambasted by a fringe group on a moral stance she took, a stand where positive change was imminent if implemented. I also had trouble in garnering support from the groups that supported my ideology. They refused to show support in fear of jeopardizing their tax exempt status. So my "Breaking the Chains Off Toledo" slogan was adopted with no elaboration to the chains I referred to, which were the spiritual chains of bondage.

After the appropriate number of signatures was validated and I received word that my name was going to appear on the primary ballot, I hit the campaign trail with as much zeal and vigor as I could muster. The field of twenty-two candidates was to be narrowed to twelve in the primaries, who then ran off against each other for the six open At-Large council seats. The six successful candidates then represented the legislative interests of the entire City of Toledo for the next four years. Six occupants of the positions were running for another term, thereby securing incumbent status which automatically gave them an upper hand due to name recognition. The remaining challengers were left with the task of convincing the electorate that they were more able in addressing the issues that face the city than the prior occupants who had at least four years of experience.

Statistical odds of unseating incumbents prevailed, as most were able to avoid major controversy and self-defeating actions, which precipitate the ouster of incumbents. Understanding the reality of this factor probably holding true, from the onset of my campaign, I held fast to my utopian ideal that if I conveyed a message more concisely than the incumbents, the electorate must grant me the privilege of serving them in an elected position. May through Election Day of 2005 was a frenzy of shaking hands at the numerous local festivals throughout the summer on the weekends, campaigning door-to-door during the week, and hosting motivational meetings to get people excited about spreading the message that I had a plan to bring progress and prosperity back to Toledo.

I arranged a few days in advance for several of my most dedicated workers to accompany me to the next festival sponsored by a community organization or a Catholic Church. We wore our "Breaking the Chains Off Toledo" T-shirts, loaded the car up with yard signs, and headed off to our first festival stop of the day. Upon arrival we would post a few signs in the grass around the festival location amongst the sea of other signs. We then posted ourselves. My volunteers held my slogan banner at strategic locations at the entrance of the venue so that every single person passing by was sure to notice and for us to offer a flyer to any interested hand. I extended a handshake, a smile, and then a request that they vote for Ernie Berry in the upcoming election.

The only thing more difficult for me than walking is standing in a stationary position. I tottered around as if I had already consumed the beverages offered inside the festival. Some people, I'm quite sure, were initially hesitant to recognize my sincerity. As they approached, they noticed my guide dog Calypso, listened to my sales pitch and recognized I was not intoxicated, but that I was genuine in my campaign endeavors. The message more often than not was received well as reflected in the primary election later that September.

The door-to-door campaign took a great toll on my body.

Not only did I walk through countless unfamiliar neighborhoods with sidewalks that were in disrepair, I also had to walk up on porches with steep steps and no hand rails. It did not matter how many times I unexpectedly tripped over a slab of sidewalk that was raised by tree roots, causing me to scrape my hands, elbows, and knees as I bounced off the sidewalk. Nor did it matter how many porches I fell up or off of, sometimes twisting an ankle. Every time I was met at the door by somebody who enthusiastically listened to my message and informed me that, "It's nice to have some new ideas," and graciously assured me that they would cast their vote for me during the primaries, I was rejuvenated. It fueled my fury in pressing through the pain to reach as many people as possible prior to the primaries. As the amount of campaign literature printed and distributed, as well as physical contacts with people reached into the thousands, I began thinking to myself that there was a very real possibility that I might be successful which bolstered my determination.

One Sunday afternoon I was walking through a neighborhood in the North End of Toledo with one of my most devout supporters. I was stopped by a police officer who informed me, "There was a report of a highly intoxicated person loitering in the neighborhood with a pit bull and I was dispatched to check it out." I was aware of the tendency for people to confuse Calypso with a pit bull based on her markings, as well as the dilemma of a misunderstanding of drunkenness due to my staggering gait, so I calmly explained the situation along with my campaign pitch. I handed him my identification card along with a campaign flyer. After reviewing the information, he passed it back to me and I took the opportunity to summarize my platform and ultimately secure his vote.

I hosted campaign meetings frequently where I assembled people who identified strongly with the methodology that I espoused of municipal management. We would primarily do two things at these meetings: strategize on how to most effectively campaign to win and work on assembling literature. We took into consideration the festivals, ranking them according to how many people were expected to attend each. This allowed us to talk to as many citizens as possible. If there were so many venues occurring simultaneously so as to prevent my personal attendance to all, a group went to pass out flyers and to talk with people. We also assembled yard signs, printed flyers, and addressed envelopes at these meetings. All the essential motions were adhered to in any winning campaign, fueled by high energy.

On the night of the primaries, I expectantly awaited the results from the Board of Elections thinking it to be a victory to advance to the general election. I had purposely run as an independent because I did not want to be slave to a party when I was elected. However, I knew that it was very difficult to even make it past the primaries without the endorsement of one of the major parties. I did not desire to depart from the principle of independence, even if it meant imminent defeat. Needless to say, I was jubilant when the final results showed that I had secured the twelfth spot. I made it through by the skin of my teeth, but the results were attributable to hard work, perseverance, and, of course, divine providence. The next morning, as I contemplated the campaign for the real deal, I became acutely aware of how difficult it would be to move into the top six from the twelfth position. Instead of allowing the notion of impossibility stand in my way, I became motivated to work harder in this next stage of the campaign to bridge the gap.

While I was having my internal bi-annual baclofen pump serviced, Cheri informed me that the battery that operated the system was failing and the unit needed to be replaced in the near future. She scheduled an appointment with Dr. Geiger who had installed the pump four years earlier. When I met with him a few days later, he ordered an X-ray of the catheter in my spinal cord to assure that it was in place.

I had never realized that the catheter was susceptible to slipping out of place. Having been brought to my attention, I was now aware that the clicking I felt and heard in the lower lumbar region of my spinal column may have been the result of the catheter wiggling out of place. I certainly hoped that this was not the case, as it meant that the entire system would have to be replaced and not just the pump, extending my hospital stay. I quickly scrolled back in my memory over all the activity that may have caused the catheter to dislodge from position. I thought of all the twisting and turning involved in my exercises, the perpetual falling involved in walking, and the endless turning and contorting involved in positioning myself to have a tolerable night's rest. It didn't take long to realize that it was highly probable that the needle needed re-insertion. I didn't worry however, and decided that if the X-ray reflected that it had been displaced, then it was going to be handled in the appropriate manner so there was no sense fretting. With this attitude, I walked across the street to the X-ray lab for my photo shoot.

Dr. Geiger's nurse contacted me after he had reviewed the X-rays. She informed me that the catheter appeared to be out of place and set up an appointment two weeks prior to the general elections. I tried to contest the surgery date, but the nurse informed me that the battery life of the pump was limited and needed to be replaced, plus the catheter re-inserted to restore full benefit of the medicine. They determined not to postpone the date further than it already had. This was just another obstacle that had to be worked out in the campaign.

As my surgery date arrived, I pushed extra hard on the campaign trail, knowing that I was unable to personally campaign during my hospital stay. Even still, I formulated a plan to post campaign signs in and outside my room, as well as to pass literature out and personally speak with every doctor, nurse, and visitor to obtain their vote, providing they were a Toledo resident.

The hospital staff wheeled me into the operating room; the anesthesiologist placed a mask over my face as I was speaking on the principles of good governance. The next thing I knew I was waking up in an eight by ten hospital cell. The surgery itself went smoothly. My first thought was to inform the nurses of no pain whatsoever in an attempt to be released early. That was until the full effect of the anesthesia wore off.

Three days passed and I began thinking that any more candidate forum absences resulted in jeopardizing the campaign. There was a forum hosted in the Old Orchard neighborhood the following evening that I was determined to make it to. I decided to sit up in bed for a few hours that evening and bragged to my family and the nurse how there was not so much as a hint of a headache. It was evident that I was lying based on my facial expressions, but the staff recognized my persistence and agreed to discharge me if, following the forum, I rested at home until the spinal cord incision was completely healed. Agreeing quickly to the terms and conditions before they retracted them, I began rehearsing the potential questions for the oral jousting that would occur the succeeding evening.

It was essential to keep my spinal column stationary so I attended the debate in a wheelchair to avoid risking a fall. I felt the beginnings of a spinal headache. If the pounding escalated to the point of incoherent mental thought, I might have to drop out of the debate, defeating the purpose of an early discharge. I determined the point of no return had passed; I was committed to the campaign and my supporters to not only show up to the forum but deliver a top notch performance. I eased out of the car into my wheelchair, wheeled into the forum venue and was carried down the stairs. The banging in my head intensified. By the time I was wheeled behind the candidates' table at the front of the room, my face was beet red and perspiration was dripping down my face from the stress of forcing myself to sit up rather than assuming a lying position. At times, I began questioning whether I had made a prudent decision. Sure my physical body was in attendance, but my mental condition was questionable at best. Even if the ability to hear and understand enough to formulate responses in my head was plausible, I was unsure an audible response was deliverable as talking amplified the throbbing. Fortunately the questions were expected and the art of oration was second nature so that the responses flowed with minimal mental exertion despite my feeble condition.

After the final question was asked, my dad pushed me to the back of room where I shook as many hands as I could until the throbbing was no longer tolerable and requested several gentlemen

124

to carry my chair up the steps. I was relieved when I made it to the car where I could shut my eyes. I was glad there wasn't another forum for a few nights, which would give me ample time to rest. Recovery lasted another four days after my initial discharge. My body's ability to regenerate was either slowing down with age or from the overexertion of my zealous campaigning. Whatever the case, I gingerly jumped back onto the campaign trail with less than a week to finish the race strongly.

The frenzied sprint down the home stretch of the campaign failed to push me into the top six positions. As I observed the final results on the local news station, I noted that Bob McCloskey, the representative from my home district received the second highest amount of votes. This meant that he had to vacate his third district council seat to assume the At-Large position. The eleven councilmen were to appoint a person to assume his former position until a special election could be held.

I naively thought that I was a qualified candidate to be the natural appointment to the vacated position as I was the highest vote getter from the third district. Even though the election that I had run in was an At-Large contest, my appointment was to be legitimated based on the votes from the third district which I had garnered in the election. To this effect, I constructed and hand-delivered a letter to each councilperson for their consideration in their upcoming confirmation hearing. Democratic justice mandated the conference of the post on a person who the public had an opportunity to vote for, but political polarization prevented justice from prevailing. Since I was neither a Democrat nor a Republican, I did not expect support from party affiliates rendering the decision regardless how compelling the argument. Since the composition of council was lopsidedly Democratic, and had been for decades, a more politically astute person had the understanding that the decision had been predetermined behind closed doors at the Democratic headquarters. Preservation of energy by abstaining from writing a letter and lobbying was the easy thing to do. My prediction was affirmed by the appointment of a Democrat, who the general public had never heard of and was granted incumbent status, thereby almost guaranteeing a victory when the special election occurred. I was losing confidence in the democratic process because of the partisanship in our city preventing a person unwilling to tow the party line from assuming leadership positions.

While I was observing the celebratory festivities at Gumbo's, a restaurant large enough to accommodate the supporters gathering to celebrate the victory of Carty Finkbeiner in his Mayoral contest, I was approached by Myndi Millican, a reporter for the "Free Press," who informed me that Michael Miller, the editor of the paper, wanted to meet with me. I filed his number away and set up an appointment. After being escorted back to his office located in a suite atop the Edison Building, he revealed the appealing proposal precipitating the meeting. He first congratulated me on a well run campaign by defying the odds of running as an Independent. He stated that he was duly impressed with my unique positions and platform, and my ability to communicate them in a concise and understandable way. He continued that he desired to offer the "Free Press" paper as an opportunity for me to further advance my opinions in the public arena through an opinion editorial column.

I was ecstatic; perhaps the previous grueling nine months didn't have to end in disappointment. I now had the opportunity to comment on political affairs, reminiscent of my talk-show days and continuation of the "Voice of Reason." I continued with the theme that defined the "Voice of Reason," combining common sense with humor and optimism, void of malice. As with my radio program, this approach was popular with the readers. Opinion editorialists are notoriously super-cynical and condescending towards policy makers, suggesting that if they were king of the world, all issues would be resolved. After receiving countless e-mails from readers commending my posture, I was encouraged to continue in this vein until resigning from writing due to a conflict of interest.

I unexpectedly received a call from the Chair of the Republican State Committee, who quickly identified himself and stated that he had followed my city council campaign. He proceeded to inform me that he was looking for viable candidates to run against entrenched Democrat incumbents throughout the state of Ohio. I immediately realized this meant that he was asking me to run against Peter Ujvagi, the state representative in the forty-seventh district. I asked him if he thought it was worthwhile of my time as the district was so democratic and loved Peter Ujvagi and his theory of government. Most voters just blindly pull the lever for him explaining why he ran unopposed so many times. He replied that if I worked as hard as I did in my citywide campaign that it was plausible for me to unseat him. Although I knew the odds were squarely against me, I identified with the optimistic train of thought and informed him that I'd have to think it over and talk to my campaigners in determining support of another endeavor.

After discussing the proposition with my most dedicated supporters, they agreed that the campaign was more manageable given the smaller voting population with the forty-seventh district, but agreed that the only possibility of victory was feasible with significant monetary and technical support from the state party in Columbus. As the deadline for filing petitions approached, and the third call inquiring as to my decision came, I agreed to run if financial support from the state party was committed. He agreed and stated that the committee was sponsoring a training day in which the Republican candidates from around the state assembled in Columbus for a training session geared to equip people to run winning campaigns in the early spring. Hearing this, I finally agreed to fill out petitions and suited up for another campaign.

Having officially entered the race, I wrote my final article in the paper, "I Won't Fiddle While Rome Burns," where I explained my civic obligation in maximizing my ability to facilitate change in an economically delayed region which found me in the precarious position of running for yet another political office to fulfill that mandate. I soon realized that this would be a campaign predicated on raw political opportunism by the state party. A better use of my time in the continuation from the bully pulpit of my editorial articles was preferable. Upon arrival in Columbus for the campaign training day, I quickly realized after all my requests for help were rejected, that the central committee was going to do absolutely nothing to aide me in leveling my assault against a political god in the Toledo area. I realized the party merely convinced me to place my name on the ballot as a preventative measure against allowing Peter Ujvagi from distributing his donations from his campaign treasury around the state to aide fellow Democrats in unseating Republicans. Realization that I was being sacrificed like a pawn in a chess match finally struck me. Refusing to besiege a fortified palace with a BB gun, the extent of this campaign was a mere trip to the Board of Elections to indicate how I would like my name to appear on the ballot as well as filing the financial statements.

Thoroughly disgusted with politics from the rejection of my application to be appointed to the vacant district council seat after a citywide, heartfelt campaign by the Democrats and secondly the political profiteering the State Republicans gained at my expense in tarnishing my claim of independence, I decided that any further engagement in politics was unlikely. I began to question if I had squandered a year of my life, abandoning a job opportunity in Washington D.C. in exchange for a year of hard labor with nothing to show. This unsettling feeling was squashed with another unexpected telephone call from Perlean Griffin, the Director of the Department of Affirmative Action and Contract Compliance with the City of Toledo; she requested that I come to city hall to meet with her the next day.

The next morning I woke excited for some unexplained reason and dressed in one of my best suits as if heading for an interview. I wondered what Mrs. Griffin wanted to talk with me about, but if she had an open position I was determined to put my best foot forward. With that in mind, I printed off my updated resume and started out the door towards downtown. When I walked into the suite on the nineteenth floor of Government Center, I was met by Mrs. Griffin's secretary who ushered me to the corner office. We exchanged the usual salutations, followed by a discussion of our families' wellbeing.

She started discussing the role of the Department of Affirmative Action and Contract Compliance in the operation of city government. She explained the four primary functions of the office as including: administration of the Affirmative Action plan, where the city was expected to maintain and work towards a workforce reflective of the greater population; investigation of Equal Employment Opportunity complaints, where objective investigations were conducted in determining non-discrimination in personnel action; Contract Compliance, where all municipal contracts were reviewed to determine adherence to Ohio State and federal law. The final function she reviewed with me was the Americans with Disabilities Act Coordinating role. This function entailed administration of the law as it relates to the Americans with Disabilities Act. Reviewing Human Resource policies and procedures in assuring that hiring, promotional, transfer, and termination practices adhered to the Acts' guidelines was the major function. Investigations of concerns raised by employees or supervisors were to be investigated in a legal context. Provisions of reasonable accommodations for temporarily or permanently disabled employees were to be determined through this position. The administrator also serves as a conduit from the community to the administration by sitting on the Mayor's Commission on Disabilities, a board comprised of executives whose non-profit organizations serve the disabled community, as well as consumers who were disabled themselves to provide direction from "first-hand knowledge" to the commission. This function coupled with constant communication with citizens voicing concerns facing the disabled population enabled the administration to respond to community concerns expeditiously through the direction of the ADA Coordinator.

After a detailed discussion of the necessity of this function, Mrs. Griffin indicated that the position was currently vacant at which point she extended the offer for me to join the administrative team. I suddenly realized all the emotionalism surrounding my feelings of rejection after my defeat in the At-Large race, the unsuccessful plea to be considered for the vacancy of the third district council seat, and the use and abuse of my zealousness for political servitude by the state Republican party were merely distractions at the door which was opened due to my diligence. God impressed upon me that although my imagination gave me a vision to be willing to serve Toledo as an At-Large Councilman, then a District Councilman, and finally a State Representative, the greater position was to be assumed in an administrative position which brought greater responsibility, effectiveness, and compensation. I realized that God multiplied my vision providing I pursued goals with godly intentions and direction.

After working as the ADA Coordinator for several months and as the financial condition of the City's budget became more evident, positions were cut and eliminated within the office, and responsibilities were redistributed. There was an expectation that the department would do the same amount of work despite cut-backs; this resulted in an increase of my responsibilities from strictly ADA to assisting with contract compliance and any function in the office.

Chapter 8

The Project of a Lifetime

When my parents moved to Oswald Street on the East Side of Toledo in 1981, there was an immaculate house just a few houses down the street. It was a large twin-plex built in 1885. An older lady owned the house; she was seen out tending her flower gardens lining the large porch on nice days or simply rocking in front of the large picture window. There were two large concrete lions that sat guard on both sides of the cement steps.

When the lady passed away her son inherited the house and sought profit from the size of the building by converting it into a four unit apartment complex. After he moved out of the city, he subdivided each apartment in half again to make eight living areas. He eventually grew tired of the rental property and sold the parcel to a real estate investment group which successfully had the property re-zoned resulting in a sixteen unit rooming house.

Each room of the original house became a separate living space with a stove, refrigerator, a few metal cabinets and a twin size bed. Several of the more luxurious rooms were equipped with their own bathrooms, but the majority of the rooms didn't have such facilities, so subsequently the renters had to utilize communal commodes. There were four sub-standard units in the basement with cement floors and no windows. One master suite was located in the attic, equipped with such amenities as its own bathroom, cooking area, and more floor space than the lower level rooms.

Maintenance for the manager amounted to nothing more than rolling a fresh piece of carpeting over a cigarette burnt, filthy carpet left by a former tenant in preparation for a replacement patron. Occasionally a fresh coat of paint, paneling, or a drop ceiling was installed to mask marks or holes left by tenants. As windows were broken, sheets of particle board were nailed up decreasing the size of the openings allowing for the installation of smaller, cheaper, mobile home windows from a scrap yard. The building was struck by lightning causing a fire; then a moon roof was installed from a car to fill the hole chopped in the attic by the firefighters who combated the fire.

As the property continued to function in that capacity, the appearance of the building as well as the quality of tenants deteriorated. Within a few years, as tenant vagabonds moved in and out on a monthly basis, the building digressed into a house of ill-repute. Soon drug dealers, abusers, and prostitutes found this location conducive for peddling their products. An ambulance was at the location responding to a drug overdose, or police were dispatched to the premises on a regular basis.

Eventually the types of activities occurring in the neighborhood where the Berry's lived became more than bearable. Drugs and prostitution were the prerogative of the free-willed adults residing there. They were crimes that were a drain on society, but as long as the majority of citizens were not directly affected they tended to be overlooked. However, knowledge of a more serious crime soon surfaced. The occupant in one of the basement apartments was a pedophile actively molesting young victims. The Boys' and Girls' Club steps were located directly across the street. To have a crack house in the neighborhood because the authorities refuse to shut it down due to the property tax revenue flowing into the public coffers was one thing. But when innocent victims are at risk, the atrocity is substantially elevated. So the Berrys prayed fervently to the One who intervenes on behalf of those incapable of defending themselves. Subsequently the building was shut down and condemned within six weeks.

The property stood vacant for the following two years attracting loiterers. Windows were broken out, resulting in people regaining entry into the building. Things were returning to the old operating status as it lingered on the demolition list. One day a note was posted on the front door indicating that the building was to be sold in an absolute auction on May 15, 2006.

The foundation and structure of the building were still in sound condition, so it had the potential of being restored to a nice home. It was more beneficial for the neighborhood to have somebody fix up the property, preferably for primary occupancy, rather than having the city demolish it and end up with a vacant lot of high weeds and long grass to take its stead. The contingency was who bought the property. If it fell into the hands of another slumlord, the original issues were bound to crop up again. I waited in expectant anticipation for auction day to observe the destiny of this once grand edifice.

I walked down the street on auction day to find the auctioneer getting ready to leave. She informed me that approximately a dozen people walked through the building and found it in such disrepair that not a single bid had been registered. At this time, my mind started to race. If nobody had bid and it was an absolute auction that meant a bid of a dollar was the highest. I had a general idea of what was entailed in restoring the building due to my extensive background in helping my father on his projects. This seemed to be the deal of a lifetime. I proceeded to ask her that if I offered a dollar if that would be the highest bid. She responded, "Yes." I then asked if there were any back taxes or liens on the property. She checked the files and affirmed that there were. My final question was that if I offered a dollar for the property with the stipulation that I would only purchase the property if the title company was successful in negating the back taxes and liens, was that an acceptable proposal. She agreed and added she had never had a prior sale of a dollar. I signed on the dotted line with confidence that I was meant to be this home's new owner.

A few weeks went by and I was beginning to think that the title company was unsuccessful in negotiating the waver of the back taxes. I received a call from Emily who identified herself as being an employee of Metropolitan Title Company. We set up an appointment to sign the closing paperwork for the purchase of my house. She informed me that the contractual obligations which were specified several weeks prior were satisfied and they were now ready to proceed.

I arrived at the office with a check for the specified amount given during a phone conversation, which I assumed was the amount of the closing cost. The receptionist seated me in a conference room. When the representative came in to discuss the nature of the agreement she informed me that when the judge had ordered the owners of the property to sell the house, he had mandated that they apply $500 towards the sale of the property due to its incredible state of disrepair. After the paperwork was signed, the house was purchased for $1. The title transfer cost $166.53 and the title company handed a check over to me for $332.47—the amount of the check I thought I owed them. Trying to hold back a grin, I asked a rhetorical question whether there was a key to the house. She laughed and said of course not.

On the bus ride home I pondered the potential opportunities for this project. I was in possession of the most dilapidated property on the East Side of Toledo, but with time and a little elbow grease, it was restorable. This served as the median through which I demonstrated to people that I was capable of transformative action in the city that I was desirous to serve.

I asked my dad and a friend, Carl Conine, to come with me to open up the house for the first time. After all, who knew if there were any living creatures inside? We notice that there was a board that had been pried off a basement window and the glass knocked out. Somebody was utilizing the living space during its vacancy. I stationed myself outside the open window while my father and Carl walked through the house. They removed a board from one of the back doors. The door fell off the hinges; the lady was right, a key wasn't necessary! My dad descended in front of Carl with a flashlight to illuminate the basement steps. My dad turned his head toward Carl to ask a question and saw that Carl had a gun pointed over his shoulder. He cried, "Hold on, Carl, you should be in front of me!" and they quickly switched positions. Fortunately, there was nobody inside because if they made it past Carl, I was waiting at the opening of the only escape route armed with a two-by-four.

When the house was deemed safe to enter, I surveyed the pitiable conditions for the first time. The house was worse than Hollywood's portrayal of drug houses in movies. A putrid odor permeated the atmosphere as I stepped across the threshold. My father walked in front of me serving as my guide since it was unfamiliar territory; he described the layout of the house. Thick leather gloves were necessary during the initial clean up phase due to the drug and prostitution paraphernalia that was scattered about. Any attempt to describe the horrendous condition prior to my acquisition of the house would be woefully inadequate and futile; suffice it to say that I had my work cut out for me and it took months to clean up the mess and rebuild.

I commenced the project by cleaning out the garage to allow the house to be aired as the smell lingered in my taste buds even after showering following a day's work. I had bagged up a few dozen bags of garbage when I was approached by a man who identified himself as John. He asked to take a rolled up chain linked fence for recycling. I instantly had an epiphany. A mutual, beneficial scenario might be worked out with John -- one that allowed him to cash the scrap metal in to put food on his table and help me by expediting the cleanup effort. I quickly showed him the contents of the garage prior to locking up and extended my proposition of permitting him free reign in hauling away scrap metal and keeping the money he received as long as he helped me by removing other large objects from the house. He eagerly responded positively because as far as he saw, there was a few hundred dollars worth of scrap in the garage. I retorted to him, "Then wait until you see the gold mine in the house!" We agreed to meet the next day to begin emptying the garage.

True to his word, John came rambling down the alley in his beat up truck at the appointed time. As he started loading his truck, I continued bagging garbage in the house. When he was finished he shouted for me to come help him start his truck. I wasn't quite sure what he meant and he explained that his truck had to be rolling backwards for his engine to turn over. I did not quite understand, but I stood next to him, place my hands on the front bumper and began pushing alongside of him. As the truck started building up momentum, he sprinted up to the driver's side door, hopped inside and turned the ignition. With this he shouted that he would see me tomorrow and departed.

When he pulled up the next day, I inquired as to the method that we had used to start his truck. He stated that his starter was bad and the cost of fixing it was a few hundred dollars and until he had the money this was how he had to start the truck. He added that it could be problematic if he stalled in traffic and needed a "back" push. I laughed to myself as I visualized John having to do this. I spurred him on by saying that after he cleared out the scrap mine, he'd be able to fix his truck.

The garage was cleared after a few trips to the scrap yard. John moved into the house where I had been piling musty furniture and mattresses into a mountainous heap outside. My dad and I drug the large pieces of furniture out to the alley to be gathered by the refuse collectors. We burned anything that was comprised of wood or flammable composite in a barrel provided by a neighbor. On a good weekend, I placed a dozen or so large pieces of furniture out for collection accompanied with numerous garbage bags. While bagging and dragging, I maintained a roaring fire with flames often shooting above the garage. I was grateful for unlimited trash pickup and for neighbors who didn't call the fire department!

John and I worked side by side for a month before the house was cleared. A conservative estimate would be that he made thirty trips. He hauled away dozens of stoves, refrigerators, metal cabinets, sinks, three furnaces and hundreds of feet of non-reusable metal pipe. John stopped in front of the house and told me that he profited over $1,500. As he got in his truck to leave, I noted that I did not have to help him start his truck. He yelled out the window as he drove off that he finally fixed it.

I acknowledged that the blessings were to be passed on to benefit others in need. I realized that the attainment of a property at such a low acquisition price was a direct result of my positive response to an offertory opportunity. A few months prior an evangelist had shared at our church. I had been blessed and encouraged by his ministry throughout the years and felt prompted to give an offering. I gave an amount that was not within my budget. If financial assets are insufficient to meet the need, they must become the seed. As the gift is then taken to bless others, the principle of giving mandates that greater dividends be paid back to the one who initially gave, especially if the offering is sewn with a cheerful heart and sincere intentions. As long as I continued adhering to this principle, I always received more than what I gave.

The man hours in labor which John gave, not out of compulsion, far exceeded the dollar amount that I would have received had I horded the recycling revenue. This was the first of many instances where a direct relationship between generous giving led to an exponential receipt in return. This concept became the life-blood of the project. I soon realized that forward progress was not sustainable unless I first took much needed money for the project and consecrated it to the work of the Heavenly Kingdom to allow God to multiply that gift two or three times. Every time I was faced with a costly purchase of tools, materials, or labor, the only thing I needed to do was give an extra offering in addition to the amount I rightfully owed to God and the purchase price of that commodity miraculously decreased so that the amount saved was several times greater than my gift.

Following the clearing out phase where all 5,000 square feet of the house was eliminated of clutter, the proverbial onion had to be peeled. The layers and layers of dropped ceiling, paneling, drywall, plaster and carpeting had to be taken out so modern electrical, plumbing, and duct work could be installed. I suited up in my work coveralls directly after work, donning gloves, mask, and goggles, scurrying from room to room with a sledge hammer and crow bar tearing everything down to the original studs. I worked furiously until ten o'clock, building debris piles substantial enough to fill the dumpsters I had ordered for the weekends.

On Saturday mornings, I met the truck driver who would roll the forty cubic yard dumpster off the back of the dual winch truck in the location that was most convenient for the area of the house we were clearing out that day. My father soon joined me to help direct the kids who came one by one, usually five or six in all, to the dumpster filling parties which became a weekly ritual for three months. I directed them inside the house to make sure they were taking things to the appropriate destination whether it be the back alley for trash pickup, the burn barrel, or the dumpster. My dad stationed himself at the dumpster to assure everything was flat and tightly packed for maximum usage.

I paced myself to load a dumpster per weekend with debris knocked down from my weekly demolition. This entailed setting up a piece of scaffolding and straddling the plank with my legs dangling. I reached overhead to the ceiling with the crow bar and would rip the lattice and plaster down. It crashed down around and on top of me. Fortunately, my hardhat held up throughout the demolition phase of the project. When I had cleared that area, I jumped off the scaffold and repositioned it beneath a section of ceiling where the plaster had not been removed, climbed back up and repeated the motions. Moving consistently throughout the room, I was able to assure that all the plaster was removed despite not being able to see. An indication of a room's completion was when the scaffold was adjacent to the spot where I had started. I disassembled the pieces of the scaffold, pushed them through the sixteen inch opening between the studs and re-assembled the sections to repeat the process in the next room.

With the clearing out and demolition phase complete, it was time to commence with rebuilding the house. To begin this phase, I went downtown and pulled the necessary building permits for the city to periodically inspect work quality. When the permits were clearly posted, work began. For this phase, I relied heavily on my dad's advice. I asked an electrician friend to install the electrical meter; Carl was in charge of plumbing, while my dad and I rebuilt the interior walls.

We deduced the original layout of the building and began threading the electrical wiring through the building. There were a few ground rules to adhere to when wiring a building. A certain number of electrical plugs were permitted to be placed on one circuit. The locations for the boxes in each room were mapped out, the holes were drilled and the wires run. Before long, I had the knack of it and began wiring entire rooms by myself. Only through God's help can a blind guy do electrical wiring that passes inspection.

One day returning home for my city job I walked through a lake of standing water in front of my house. I knew immediately what the issue was. The previous day a city crew had come to turn on the water main. Carl had finished with the plumbing and I was eager to have running water in the house. The issue was subterranean; the hundred-year-old galvanized pipe which carried the water from the main waterline underneath the street to the house had burst. Knowing what it would entail to remedy the problem, I prayed that the break was on the city's side. A simple test confirmed that it was somewhere underneath my house, so I began preparing myself mentally for the grueling task of digging a trench to lay a new waterline.

I had experience in replacing waterlines; one had burst a few years earlier at one of my dad's properties, which was also built at the end of the nineteenth century. My house was similar in that both properties didn't have a full basement. So if the waterline breaks, one has to dig a three-foot deep by fifty-foot long trench underneath a crawl space! To intensify the challenge there was about a two-foot clearance from the dirt to the floor joists, which caught the tip of my shovel throwing me off rhythm. If I was lucky, a half a dozen scoops in a row with the shovel were taken before hitting my hands or head on the joists.

My dad's line conveniently burst in the middle of summer when I was in high school. Time was not an issue and it took nearly two weeks to dig the trench. This time a new semester in my graduate school program was about to start and I didn't have time to play in the sand box. I set a tentative deadline to motivate myself to complete the back-breaking task in less than five days. This meant working until after the sun went down, which wasn't a factor since light did not reach the crawlspace and besides that I didn't need light for digging. My back ached, not just from the normal muscle fatigue, but also from where my catheter was fused with my spinal cord. I refused to allow this to slow me down because I had a deadline to meet. After two days and evenings of nonstop digging, the trench was finally complete and the new line was ready to be installed. A team was assembled to push the three-quarters inch by seventy-five foot solid copper line in position. It took a few hours to push it underneath the sidewalk, past three foundation walls, and to maneuver it around immovable objects.

After the various inspectors placed their stamps of approval on the infrastructure of the house, drywall was next on the construction list. I purchased three hundred sheets of drywall and had them delivered to my garage. The blessing of God was observed in the purchase price of this commodity, as with everything else.

I didn't harbor the savings, but rather hired an extra helper to hang and mud the drywall. After a few weeks of this, one side of the twin-plex began to look like an inhabitable dwelling. The apartment was equipped with updated electricity, ample water pressure and a new heating and ventilation system powered by a 92% efficiency, one-hundred thousand BTU furnace, which was graciously given to me by the roofer.

The Final Outcome

Had I known the labor, materials, and excruciating headaches involved in tackling such a project, recognition that a dollar was too high of a price for the building was the common sense response. However, when the property was mine and the nuisance letters started percolating from the Department of Neighborhoods, I had to follow the project through to the end. As with prior, seemingly insurmountable obstacles, these letters stimulated my imagination to not only fix the property up to the standards mandated, but to exceed them as my natural tendency was to exert maximum performance under pressure.

Aggravating expenditures such as permit fees were a way in which the Division of Code Enforcement maintained a consistent revenue stream throughout my project. At the beginning of each stage of a project, I went downtown to pay a hundred dollars to the city to have them send an inspector out to tell me that work completed was up to code. The largest unexpected expenditure came in the form of a water lien that was not processed until a year after I maintained possession of the property. This lien was for six years of water bills that the previous owner neglected to pay, costing me over $1,300. The tax situation was equally as trying; I found myself being taxed for a commercial property that was valued by the county for higher than what the real estate value was, even after I advised them that the status of the property had changed. In essence the physical explanation was that the city and county governments observed an opportunity to nickel and dime an unsuspecting citizen out of revenue that they thought was rightfully theirs. There was a spiritual reality that Satan was using these fees, fines, and outrageous taxation measures to cause me to regret purchasing the property in the first place and to distract me from seeing the blessing which was shortly forthcoming if only I would press through these trials.

The positive benefits far exceeded the negative consequences. They included working with and influencing people to adopt and share the excitement in the restoration of the building. The completed project entailed completely gutting the infrastructure of a house of ill-repute, and rebuilding it with high quality building materials and specifications in transforming one side into a home for myself and a revenue generating apartment on the other side. The only internal, original feature indicating the pride, joy, and care in restoration of the edifice is a set of old sliding pocket doors which took hours to refurbish. As I reflect back on the progression of my house project, weighing the costs and benefits, I have concluded that the benefits have outweighed the costs. Also, I have discovered the end result of life's exceedingly difficult struggles have yielded a more pristine outcome than had I abstained from facing life's overwhelming challenges head on and have resolved to live life to its fullest.

Chapter 9

Wacky Wheelchair Woes

God will not allow me to remain bound to a wheelchair for an extended length of time as it would pose too much of a threat to the public! During the demolition phase of my house project, I struck my knee with a sledgehammer. I had neither the balance nor the coordination to use crutches. The only alternative was a wheelchair as my means of travel during the recovery phase.

I saw this temporary placement in a wheelchair as a prime opportunity to simulate an actual dependence on such a device if a permanent reliance ever was to occur. I opted to view my situation in the "cup was half full" manner -- as long as I was bound to a wheelchair I no longer had to cope with tripping over my toes every other step and all the frustration that came with walking. Since aerobic exercise wasn't possible via the EFX machine, I had to deal with increased tightness, harsher spasms, and the negative emotions that resulted.

My uncle had a wheelchair stowed away in his attic that I borrowed throughout my escapades. Although it wasn't a racing wheelchair, the speed at which I traveled was governed by how fast my arms could pump the wheels. This is where my arm strength and endurance came into play. I knew that there was a practical application for the upper body strength that God had blessed me with. Menial tasks such as bench pressing well over twice my body weight at the gym or tripling the amount of pull-ups an overly boastful athlete did in a friendly wager were no longer the only purpose in great upper body strength. Now the practical application was propelling myself in my chair as swiftly as possible from point A to point B.

The distance from home to work was now traversable faster than riding the bus. On work days, I settled into my chair and cruised down the road to work. I learned quickly to utilize the road whenever possible to avoid the upsets that resulted from hitting bumps or protruding obstacles that were prevalent in sidewalk travel. In addition, I could build up a higher rate of speed as I didn't have to worry about pedestrians in the street. Of course, common sense was used; cars weren't to be challenged and sidewalks had to be used when traveling along major streets.

Subject to my competitive nature, I saw every trip to or from work not only as a method of upper body aerobic exercise, but also a challenge to continuously top my prior personal record in the half mile sprint across the bridge. To decrease my time, shortcuts were

147

mentally mapped out, curbs were traversed without use of the appropriate curb ramps, and my muscles were pushed to the limit despite the lactic acid build up which made them scream for a break.

During these fast and furious marathons, my faithful companion Calypso took a hiatus from her usual guide dog duties to keep pace at a sizable distance of twenty feet. She was mortified of the wheels and was unsure when a crash might occur. The separation, as well as the demeanor in which Calypso was tailing me, led the majority of bystanders to mistake her for a stray.

It wasn't long before I realized that gravity was a useful accelerant when harnessed. My first real need to exploit this came in a semester when I had a class that let out thirty minutes prior to another class in which I was enrolled that was located at the opposite end of the University of Toledo's campus. Being a twenty minute trek on foot by a power walker, it was a feat to span the distance without being late for class.

There happened to be a very large hill en route between the football stadium and the recreation building that declined at a substantial slope. If I descended it without wiping out, the momentum accumulated would be great enough to carry me a sizable distance. As the top of the hill was approached, I contemplated the benefits of making it to class on time versus the exhilaration of attempting a dangerous new wheelchair speed record. Having committed my mind to this stunt, I started down the hill allowing my chair to pick up speed. The wheels shook back and forth violently if a certain speed was surpassed. To prohibit this from resulting in deceleration, I leaned over my knees assuming a more aerodynamic position and firmly grasped hold of the brackets around each wheel. The wheels stopped wobbling and I began picking up more speed. When I started passing cars, I grew concerned and realized that I had a larger problem on my hands than the shaky wheels. Stopping was not possible as my hands were busy holding the front wheels in place, so there was no way to control the brakes. I knew that if I suddenly let go of the front wheels to apply the brakes, the shaking was to resume so furiously a crash was imminent. This was one of those moments that one realizes that there's nothing to do but hold on for the ride. I prayed to make it to the bottom safely, or at least to sustain only minor bumps and bruises.

Fortunately, I made it to the bottom of the hill with momentum enough to carry me a considerable distance and made it to class on time. It occurred to me that it may behoove me to wear a safety helmet, which might come in handy when an imminent accident occurred.

Since my university office was located on the periphery of campus, which was elevated higher than the middle of campus, the gravitational pull concept in traveling from my office to central locations on campus with minimal wheel pushing due to the series of hills leading to downhill graduations was possible. Immediately outside my office was a slightly steeper slope, although not as long as the slope by the football stadium. When at the bottom of this slope, the momentum was great enough to carry me to a gradual downhill slant, which carried me another distance through a narrow passage way behind the old Field House and shot me out into the central mall area in the middle of campus. In order to hit this gradual decline coming off from the steep slope, there was about a five foot wide threshold where the asphalt met the sidewalk that disallowed for a miscalculation. In order to make this, I had to rely on the precision steering that I developed by twisting my wrists as my hands firmly clasped onto the brackets of the front wheels. I did not have a lot of time to make the decision of when to turn and how sharply to turn as I was still traveling at a high rate of speed during the approach. I did not see visually where the asphalt and sidewalk met. I was forced to rely on timing, a unique ability to detect inanimate objects through a quazi-echolocation mechanism and luck.

After the successful transition onto this narrow passage way, I was faced with the issue of how to avoid pedestrians, so during this stretch I would make a lot of noise, yelling, "Watch out, blind guy in wheelchair coming through!" If this didn't serve as an adequate warning, I would pray for the pedestrians' safety and divine intervention in avoiding a collision. When I made it to the final plateau, I resumed pushing in the direction of my destination and called for Calypso who was galloping somewhere in the distance, maintaining her safety margin to avoid any possibility of her involvement in a mishap.

During one of my routine trips down the hill previously described, I reached the bottom of the first large hill, coasted along at a high rate of speed for a distance, and as I approached the transition point from the asphalt to the sidewalk, I sensed something obstructing my path. As I rushed up on it I barely made it out; it looked like a box truck. A decision had to be made quickly regarding the appropriate action to take. There was perhaps twenty feet in from of me when I first noticed the obstacle. There wasn't time to turn, gradually come to a stop, or do anything that would avoid direct impact other than immediately screeching to a halt.

Without hesitation I grabbed the two back wheels as tight as possible. I felt the wheels skidding under me and the chair losing traction. It skidded and then lurched. The next thing I knew I was hurtled into the air and landed about five feet in front of the truck. I immediately crawled back to my toppled wheelchair, uprighted it, and hopped back in the seat. When I reached down I discovered that all four tires detached from the wheels due to the abrupt stop. Apparently the design of the chair wasn't meant to withstand such an ordeal. Pushing everything to the max had become one of my core values and I believe I discovered the maximum utility for a wheelchair that wasn't built like a tank!

I knew that the tires were much like bicycle tires in that they were designed to be taken on and off, although probably not through the method that I just employed. I feverishly started stretching the hard rubber to get them back in the grooves, it's a good thing that I have strong hands or else I would have had to take it into the wheelchair mechanics for a wheel alignment. Meanwhile I was hoping nobody was watching me or worst yet witnessed the ordeal, I did not want to explain the decisions that precipitated such a predicament. It was a nice day in the middle of the semester, on a college campus with more than twenty thousand students; of course there were witnesses! Just as I was thinking this, several guys ran up and exclaimed, "Dude, that was awesome, you were airborne. Are you all right?" To which I replied that I was okay and it was, "just another day in the neighborhood." They proceeded to help with the rest of the repairs to my chair and when complete, I thanked them and was on my way.

Another one of my core principles is not to limit myself to the performance of only one activity when I can multi-task with equivalent effectiveness and quality. For the most part this methodology results in maximal efficiency and increased leisure time. However on several occasions the result caused me to wonder if it was truly worth it. One of these occasions occurred during my intense preparation for an Organizational Theory class examination. I arrived downtown from campus and was wheeling myself while listening to my theoretical textbook on my laptop crossing the Martin Luther King Bridge to my home. This allowed me to travel home, study, and get my upper body aerobic exercise.

I took a moment and set my computer up to read the file that I needed, plugged in my ear phones, closed the lid to my laptop with a piece of cloth between the screen and the keyboard to prevent the computer from shutting off, zipped the heavily padded bag up so only the wire to the earphones were protruding, and started on my way. I knew the course like the back of my hand having traveled it countless times, thus I was able to devote my attention to the subject matter streaming through my head set. When it was crucial to give full attention to my surroundings, as in crossing the street, I simply flipped my ear pieces out, crossed the street, pushed them back in, called to Calypso, "Hurry up," and continued on my way.

I reached the expansion portion of the bridge, which had a slight uphill grade to the summit. There was an equally gradual downhill descent that was a prime opportunity to let gravity take over. I assumed my aerodynamic position and remained engrossed in listening to my book. The further the distance I travelled the more momentum I picked up; I was about halfway down the bridge when I felt a thud on my left side, which caused my chair to capsize tossing me onto the sidewalk. I struggled to right my chair, unfold it and jump back in before anybody noticed, being careful that my ear pieces stayed in place as not to miss any pertinent information.

I continued onward with a little more caution. I crossed the boulevard at the base of the bridge and took a nosedive. This time the front wheels dropped out from underneath me as if going directly off a curb. The rest of the chair followed landing on top of me, and I found myself in a gravel pit. Apparently a city sidewalk crew had taken up a few sections of sidewalk for repairs, and neglected to cordon off the area.

It seemed to me that there was a conspiracy amongst construction crews to neglect posting adequate signage in order to give disabled pedestrians additional trouble or to give bystanders entertainment! In either case, I found myself having to set my chair up on level ground again all the while not missing a word from my book.

As I rounded the final corner, I heard a car pull beside me and honk. I flipped out my ear pieces and the driver quickly identified himself as my neighbor, Mark.

He said, "Ernie, I was listening to my police scanner and heard that there was a wheelchair crash on the Martin Luther King Bridge and I knew it had to be you."

I replied, "You assumed correctly, but you didn't have to come looking for me, you know I'd make it home eventually."

He said, "Yeah, I just came to bail you out in case they gave you a breathalyzer and took you downtown!"

One afternoon as I was working downtown, I needed to go to the bank on my break. I knew that time was short so I left Calypso in the office as I only had fifteen minutes to wheel to the bank, take care of my business and wheel back. The banking institution was merely a block up the street from my building, so I assumed I had ample time. I took the elevator to the ground floor and quickly wheeled out to the intersection.

As I was sitting on the corner, formulating my game plan to get from Government Center to the bank while I was waiting for the light to change I knew that the faster I got to the bank, the more time I had to spend taking care of my business. I could make it to the bank rather quickly if I built up a full head of steam as soon as the light changed. The downwards slope of the ramp yielded momentum in wheeling up the slight street grade. If momentum was built up in summating the peak, increased momentum on the downhill slope was to be expected. When at the bottom, the momentum was great enough to carry me up the adjacent ramp with minimal effort, and the remaining momentum was transferable in making it to the bank in record time.

There was one underlying assumption that was necessary to make this plan work; the two ramps had to be aligned. The implications were disastrous if this wasn't the case. I soon discovered that it was a foolish blunder to make such an assumption.

The light turned green and my parallel traffic started to move. When the first car was in the middle of the intersection indicating that it was safe to cross, I heaved the chair forward with everything I had. Just five pumps and I crested the peak. I felt the chair speed up as gravity kicked in. I made two quick pumps and felt the chair instantaneously stop upon ramming the curb. I was projected about five feet forward and landed with a thud. Realizing that I had miscalculated, I brushed myself off, gathered my pride and quickly hopped back in my chair. As I passed the gawking crowd of people waiting at the bus stop, I informed them that admission was free for this circus sideshow, but I may have to charge them next time.

When it was time for my bi-annual extraction and injection of baclofen, I found myself preparing for another fun trip in the rain. My appointment was at 9:00 in the morning at St. Vincent's Medical Center on Cherry Street, a half mile up the road from Government Center. Having had my baclofen pump adjusted and filled many times, I knew how long it took to get from my house to the hospital, have the procedure, and get to work. I informed my boss of my timely arrival to work after the procedure.

I had to maintain a steady pace to coordinate my arrival at bus stops in such a way as to board the bus with minimal waiting. There was one additional factor that hindered promptness; it was raining cats and dogs. The warm temperature and elevated humidity provoked me to leave the house without a rain jacket. I proceeded to load my wheelchair by hanging my cloth lunch sack from the handles on the back of the chair, situated myself with my computer case in my lap and stripped off to my undershirt putting my dress shirt in my lunch sack so a dry over-shirt was awaiting me upon my arrival to work.

Rather than wheeling across the bridge in a torrential downpour, I thought it was advantageous to take the short trip over the river in the bus and transfer to another bus to reach my final destination. I called to Calypso to follow and left slipping and sliding towards the bus stop at the end of the street. I didn't have to wait long for the bus to arrive. The driver flipped out the ramp, I boarded, he strapped me down and we were off. I checked the time and realized that we were on schedule to make it downtown in time to catch the 19 bus that was scheduled to drive in front of the hospital at 8:30, which gave me a half hour to dry off before my appointment. We arrived at the transfer point and the driver released me. I rolled off the bus and much to my delight the 19 arrived within five minutes. This was going too smoothly. There had to be a catch; rarely had anything gone this smoothly!

The driver locked my chair down in the appropriate precautionary manner after boarding the next bus, and I observed that the driver was new. I had experience with new drivers and knew I had to treat this situation with careful strategy. I started describing exactly which stop I wanted to get off at. I explicitly requested to get off immediately before the hospital at Page Street. I reiterated the request to exhaustion. When I was finally satisfied that he was certain where I wanted to get off by the tone in his voice, I was confident he got the point.

In short order, the bus stopped and the driver called out, "This is your stop." I unstrapped myself, which was a courtesy I adopted so the drivers didn't have to get out of their seat and rolled myself down the ramp. I rolled until I was in the middle of what I assumed was Page Street and took a right hand turn. I barely saw the outline of the large building which I thought was the hospital. I rolled a hundred meters down the road and took a sharp left into the easement of the parking lot. I rolled up the incline, across the sidewalk and into the parking lot when I immediately suspected something was amiss. I heard the crunch of gravel; the hospital parking lot was asphalt. I realized the driver had dropped me off too soon. I had no idea how far I was from the hospital. The only thought that popped into my mind was that there goes my drying off period.

I rolled forward and started to turn around when I felt the chair sink and the wheels immediately lock. I frantically pushed the wheels as hard as I could and they simply spun in mud; my hands slipped off the bars of the wheels due to the rain. I thrust both hands full force into protruding metal objects on the chair which cut deep into my hands. I deduced I was stuck in the middle of a construction zone in the pouring rain with just an under shirt on and now with bleeding, stinging hands. So much for being prompt!

I heard footsteps, which I assumed belonged to a construction worker. If I got his attention, he'd free me from this mess. I started yelling, and as he walked towards me he asked, "Does your dog bite?"

I responded, "No," and asked him to help me out. He quickly pushed me out to the sidewalk. I was hoping that the driver merely dropped me off one block shy, so I wheeled in the appropriate direction and was pleased to find that was the case.

I rolled into the office, sopping wet with Calypso following like a drenched rat. The nurse was preparing my medicinal refill and I had arrived on time. She quickly distilled the area around my pump, plunged the needle in, took out the old baclofen, put in the new and off I went. I took the elevator up to the second floor to cross over Cherry Street utilizing the covered crosswalk. I wheeled to the bus shelter to catch the inbound bus. I decided to put my shirt on as I was to be minimally exposed to the elements for the short ride to my office.

After wiping off the excess water that had accumulated on

my skin, I reached around behind me to grab my shirt only to discover the sack was gone. I realized that the construction guy was not a construction worker; he was homeless and seized the opportunity to snag a free lunch! I was naive to think that a construction worker would be on the job in a downpour! At the time I was unsure of what frustrated more - the loss of my lunch or my shirt. I recalled a verse in the Bible which prompts people to hand over their tunic after a thief steals their cloak. I guess a lunch and shirt is equally applicable.

The bus had arrived and was to be downtown in five minutes. I was on schedule to arrive to work on time, but had not the proper attire. I called my mother to request her to bring a dry shirt, but she was not home. Immediately, my hyperactive mind went to work in finding potential remedies for this predicament. The answer was obvious as there was only one clothing store on the route. Located across the street from the stop that I would exit the bus was a Goodwill Store. I rolled in, grabbed a five dollar button down shirt and briefly shared the frustrations of my dilemma. The clerk left her post and returned with a rain jacket, gave it to me and advised me to wear it saying, "I can't help you out with your lunch, but this might save you some trouble in the future."

Chapter 10

Jack of All Trades, Master of Public Administration

Following my college graduation and decision to run for public office, it was necessary for me to determine which brand of graduate school to pursue. Diversification is pertinent in life's endeavors so one isn't in the position of placing all their hopes and dreams in one basket and starting over if it doesn't work out. If my council run didn't succeed, I wanted a plan on the back burner to offset lost time.

At this point in time, I had already ruled out law school. However, I was familiar with the structure of the Law School

Admissions Test and thought it challenging and desired to take it in comparing my score with the general population of law school hopefuls. A satisfactory LSAT score was a suitable substitute for the Graduate Entrance Exam required by a Master's program. The LSAT was also more appealing than the GRE because of the logic based content, the exclusion of mathematics, and it was less expensive. I found the logic model exercises of the exam to be simple. The years of strategic thought in the game of chess had prepared me well. After receiving my score on one of the most difficult exams I had ever taken, I was surprised to receive a sufficient score to be admitted to a myriad of ranking law schools around the country.

As the weeks passed and graduation grew closer, decision time drew near. I began strategically thinking about my life's goals. I desired to hold a public office; it would behoove me to have a theoretical framework to draw from when I attained such a position. The Master's program in Public Administration was an appropriate avenue to equip me with the formal education in public service. The MPA program was the only professional Master's program within the Department of Arts and Sciences at the University of Toledo where there was a continuous effort throughout the program to bridge theory and practice. The program was designed for students to enter directly into the workforce. After discussing the program with friends who were currently enrolled and ones who had graduated from the program, I filled out the paperwork and submitted the appropriate documentation for admission to the program.

I was fully engrossed in my campaign when I received acceptance into the Master's program. I didn't desire to overcommit myself to taking classes due to my campaign. I registered for a Public Policy Theory course that was beneficial in my campaign by allowing me to incorporate concepts learned in class. I was able to be more convincing with my approach to governing when talking to people. My council campaign had ended and I was writing for the "Free Press" when it came time to enroll for the next semester of classes. I registered for a Non-Profit Management elective. A few weeks into the semester I received a call from the Affirmative Action and Contract Compliance Director offering me a city position which filled my schedule to its fullest.

I was now gainfully employed with a full-time job with full benefits and tuition reimbursement. The financial burden of the graduate school tuition was resolved when I was blessed with this job. I discovered that graduate classes were scheduled at night to accommodate full-time employees. It was difficult for me to take more than one class a semester in conjunction with my job and my house project. At this point, I decided to embark upon the most daunting set of classes in the Master's program – statistics! This course was a primarily visual discipline; a minor miracle was necessary for me to pass two semesters at the graduate level. I reluctantly registered for the first class, bracing myself for hours and hours of painstaking study squinting at the formulas and symbols under my close circuit television causing head-splitting migraines. As I eased into the desk on the first night of classes, praying for God to grant me the grace to make it through these stat classes the professor walked in. To my amazement, the instructor of this class was Peg Wallace, the manager of Selection and Evaluation, who worked directly across the hall from me. This divine appointment granted me access to the instructor for personal, one-on-one tutorial sessions during my lunch hour every day both semesters. An additional blessing of rides from work to the university with Dr. Wallace eliminated the use of public transit for that leg of my journey. I realized that the nearly impossible courses were simplified with this latest divine appointment. This didn't shock me as these miracles had become commonplace in my life.

When I began the second statistics class in my fourth semester during my second year of graduate school, it crossed my mind that if I continued at this pace, it was going to take about eight years to complete my degree. Although I didn't mind the extended time as long as I maintained employment, I was used to completing projects much faster than the current forecast projected. Besides, I didn't desire to overextend myself in taking more classes due to my busy schedule and paying the upfront money that was entailed in the tuition reimbursement policy. My concern was heard by an all-knowing Lord who sent the solution in an unimaginable form that entailed nothing more than following His direction.

Due to financial difficulties, the administration of the City of Toledo was forced to make drastic budget reductions. Consequently, my position was cut from a full-time, forty hour work week to a part-time, twenty hour work week. With this reduction a loss of benefits occurred including tuition reimbursement. Another concern was that I now had to fund my real estate project with half the revenue stream. My hopes of securing even a minor loan from a lending institution, let alone a mortgage, to fuel my house project were dashed when I learned of my position cut. I had to go into super-saver mode on all fronts, as well as finding secondary employment elsewhere to jumpstart my plans.

One evening, as I was walking to the bus stop, I ran into the chair of the department and stopped for one of my long winded, cheerful discussions. As I continued on my way, I had a thought placed in my mind, "You should go apply for a graduate assistantship!" So the very next day, I stopped into the departmental building and retrieved the application from the secretary who said she wanted to see me fill a position, but she was not sure if there were any available. I quickly filled out the information and submitted it promptly, feeling it to be a time-sensitive situation. I waited about two weeks before I called the director of the program to check on the status of my application, who informed me that it looked as if all the positions were taken, but that possibly one was going to open for the spring semester. At this point, I was concerned that I may have to postpone my plans for six months as I waited. Nevertheless, I continued calling for the next few weeks to no avail in obtaining an official answer. I received a letter well into the summer, addressed from the Department of Political Science, which I assumed must be the official rejection notice. The very first word in the letter was "Congratulations," and my spirit soared. My assumption of the remaining content of the letter was correct; I was to receive a tuition waiver for all classes that I took while I was a graduate assistant, a generous stipend was to be paid for twenty hours work performed in the department, and the assistantship was valid for three semesters. When I calculated the monetary equivalence of the tuition waiver in addition to the stipend, I found the amount to be a larger sum than the amount loss due to the city's reduction of my hours. In actuality, it was a promotion through a demotion with the opportunity of completion of my degree in a more expedient time frame.

As the graduates met in the basement of the department to be assigned their responsibilities for the upcoming semester, some of the second-year assistants were assigned freshmen level classes to teach, some were assigned professors to work with on special projects, and I was assigned the responsibility of recruiting for the program where the enrollment had been in decline for several semesters. Dr. Bachelor, the chair of the department said, "I specifically chose you, Ernie, to spearhead this effort because you know everybody, and you are very well spoken so you can sell the program well!" In reality, I knew a lot of people due to my community activism, but everybody knew Calypso. Even if they didn't, they wanted to meet her, so by default I was permitted to meet many more people on account of my popular dog. To a certain extent, this contributed to the success in the campaign, but when the initial meeting was over, I had the gift of gab and sold ice to an Eskimo.

The mission was clear cut; just talk to as many upperclassmen as possible facing the decision of which graduate program to commit to and send email solicitations to students at other four-year colleges without an accredited MPA program in hopes of drawing them to our fine institution; the students should naturally flock to the program. Two weeks of precision distribution of program literature passed without as much as a nibble on the hook. People were uninterested in committing another year and a half of their lives to an academic discipline that didn't guarantee a six-figure salary with full benefits and a retirement package.

I began to realize that if I were to successfully sell the program, the program needed a hook that was more appealing to continuing students than the competition of other fields. Thinking back on my own college of choice, I chose the University of Toledo because I was permitted to take courses at UT while I was a senior in high school. Having completed my freshman year of college while most high school seniors were searching for the appropriate university, I was already committed to an institution and was not tempted to transfer lest credits were lost in the process. I began building a scheme based on the presupposition that if upperclassman attending the University of Toledo were allowed to take graduate classes in the Public Administration Program, earning both undergraduate and graduate credit, the likelihood that a full commitment to the MPA program upon graduation was greatly increased.

The proposition was primarily based on my post-secondary experience in transitioning from high school to college and by students at the university as being a method of solidifying a commitment to our program. Armed with the student survey data affirming my claim of the success of the program in increasing enrollment, I informally proposed the idea to the chair of the department, who stated, "That's a brilliant idea!" and immediately placed a call to the chair of undergraduate council to set up an appointment between he and I to allow me an opportunity to convince him of the validity of the program.

When I met with the chair of undergraduate council, I realized the difficulties involved in garnering support for a new program. Though he was the starting point, I'd have to convince many others who desired to amend the program to conform it to their traditional ideal of higher education before claiming the idea as their own. It was the typical bureaucratic process that I was familiar with, having worked for the city for two years. However, I was so convinced of the merit of the program that as long as I was persistent, regardless of who reflexively rejected the proposal because it was coming from a mere graduate student and not a tenured professor, I was confident in the acceptance of the program. Organizations are naturally resistant to policy change, which was necessary for the passage of the proposal. If the proposal languished longer than my stay as a graduate, I may not have been able to finish what I had initiated.

My non-bureaucratic mentality, which detested complication of simple solutions to remedy problems, took over. I pushed hard to direct the proposal through the pertinent channels, paying little attention to protocol, as form over function was futile. My relentless push towards implementation of the program as a viable recruitment tool resulted in the adoption of the program just weeks after my graduation. As a matter of fact, it was so well received that two more departments in addition to the Political Science department decided to adopt the measure. Decades of antiquated recruitment methodology was suddenly turned on its side and supplemented with a policy initiated by someone who was willing to think outside of the box.

In addition to my recruitment responsibilities, I was assigned to assist in teaching a freshmen level government class during my last semester of graduate school. The content of the curriculum was second nature, and keeping the lectures within the time constraints proved to be the most challenging part of the class. I assisted the professor in creating tests and quizzes to assess whether the students comprehended the material. Eighty-five students were registered for the class, creating a considerable amount of paperwork to be graded. However with the assistance of my voice-text software, I was able to breeze right through them. I also had office hours and hosted study sessions for students who needed extra help on grasping particular concepts for papers or exams. By the end of the semester, there were no students who dropped out of the class, and only a handful of unsatisfactory grades.

During the evening, while I was working twenty hours a week downtown, twenty hours a week at the university and whatever spare time I could muster on my house, I was occupied studying the theoretical components of administration. Having taken two essential core classes and two electives as a part-time student, prior to my schedule overload, I was faced with taking such classes relating to organizational, budgetary, personnel, decision-making, policy theory, and management as my remaining core classes, as well as additional elective courses chosen at my discretion.

Fortunately I had an ability to read, comprehend and regurgitate massive amounts of literature, resulting in rarely re-reading information, which was nice due to the thousands of pages of material covered over brief intervals. Furthermore, I found myself in the position of not having to take notes in class due to an impeccable ability to commit complex lecture material to memory and instantly recall the information verbatim on exam day.

I was so preoccupied with day to day activities that I failed to see the light at the end of the tunnel until I missed the deadline for graduation. My perpetual procrastination with petty things almost delayed the receipt of my diploma for another semester; which was inexcusable. My mother had notified everybody of the exact date of my graduation and my brother had secured a plane ticket from

California to Detroit. I had no idea why this problem had plagued me. I took on large projects or obstacles with all my energy without delay, for example practicing to become a chess champion, a weightlifting champion, or tackling building projects. I even started term papers at the beginning of the semester and completed them well before their deadline. However, it seemed as if I was always jeopardizing my hard work by neglecting menial things such as a follow-up phone call, sending an email, or filing a form.

A sinking feeling came over me as I was discussing graduation with the chair of the program when he asked me if I had applied prior to the deadline for graduation. First of all, I was unaware of an application process; I thought that after a few years of graduate school walking down the aisle was automatic. Secondly, if there was a deadline, I likely missed it as it was already two weeks until graduation day. As he brought up the form on his computer, he informed me that the deadline was two months prior. Without hesitation, I asked him to print the form and sign it. I then hurried down the steps to my office to fill out my portion, and trekked across the field to drop the application off at the graduate school as fast as possible.

As I wrestled with the thought that I might not be able to graduate due to the missed deadline, I was confident that my plea would successfully prompt the office to expedite the paperwork. Realizing that even the most efficient bureaucracy could not process paperwork on such short notice, I was once again reminded that insignificant dilemmas, even the ones instigated by my own neglect, were minor for God who has all things under His control. As I pondered all the trying times, minor and major, and how they all worked for good in my life, the only explanation was divine intervention. I had a suspicion that a colossal issue of enormous magnitude was just around the corner which would make every trial to date seem like a mere molehill. Finally, I made it to the commencement ceremony and was awarded a Master of Public Administration Degree, a Certificate in Non-profit Administration and a Certificate in Municipal Management to serve as tokens symbolizing completion of my academic achievements.

Chapter 11

Facing the Giants

Cell Phone Pre-Test

Significant trials where patient endurance was necessary in passing the test foreshadowed many substantial breakthroughs in my life. One of these tests came in the form of a series of outrageous cell phone bills that seemingly had no purpose until the real test reared its head shortly after the resolution of the pre-test.

At the time, I had an account where I paid three cell phone lines on a family plan with the T-Mobile company: a line for myself, one for my sister and another for my mother and father to share. The agreed upon conditions placed on the usage of the service was simple, nobody was to exceed one-third of the thousand minutes of the plan. This was adhered to for the initial years of the arrangement. Then my sister exceeded her allotted minutes three months in a row and despite my verbal warnings, she continued to do so. I proceeded to ask her how to remedy the situation. She responded by informing me of a feature that "everybody except her" utilized that would minimize her talk time on the phone. Text messaging was a popular way to communicate where unlimited usage of the service was available for only ten dollars more a month.

Weeks passed and mail piled up due to my hectic schedule of being enrolled in my final semester in my master's program, putting the finishing touches on my dollar house in preparation for renting it out, plus various other activities. After observing a second quarter-inch thick packet from T-Mobile, my mother decided to open it, as she suspected it was probably important. She went to the first packet and opened it as well. She exclaimed, "Ernie, these are your cell phone bills and you owe over $2,200!" Without hesitation, I had customer service on the phone. A representative answered and I briefly explained the situation and asked to speak with her manager. I informed the manager about the dilemma of the negligence of the customer service representative three months prior failing to place unlimited text-messaging capacity on the requested line. My sister, as well as I, assumed that she had unlimited texting since that was what I had requested and she proceeded to send over 10,000 text messages. However, the representative had only added a 400 text message limit. Therefore, the system tracked the text messages as overage charges to the tune of thirty five cents a message. The end result was two ridiculously expensive monthly statements in a row. I explained that my sister was not permitted to text that amount of messages without her having unlimited texting ability on her line, which was what I requested three months prior. The manager stated that he was only permitted to deduce the actual course of events based on the notes of the customer service representative, and according to the representative's notes she had noted that I indicated placing only 400 text messages on the line. The manager said that I was responsible for the overages.

I spent hours conversing with several managers constructing the argument in various ways in hopes that one of them was reasonable in seeing the true picture. But it was to no avail. I resolved to ask an attorney friend in the morning what course of action to take in acquiring restitution. I called my long-time friend Peter Silverman the next morning who advised me to draft a letter detailing the situation with an ultimatum to make restitution within seven days of the receipt of the letter or legal action was going to be taken. Weeks passed without so much as an acknowledgement from the company that they had received my letter. Meanwhile, January was rapidly approaching when property taxes were due and a $1,100 delinquent water bill from the previous slumlord's evasion was expected to appear. The unexpected outflow of over $2,000 from my bank account and this second large bill (which I was not responsible for), caused me to question whether to proceed in purchasing an adaptive computer system for my mother for Christmas for her to utilize in assisting her in teaching students with learning disabilities. The cost of the entire system was more than $3,000, which was now a large sum given the unexpected situation.

A week prior to Christmas, I received a call from an

executive level manager from T-Mobile who indicated that she received my letter and was going to listen to the recorded conversation between the customer service representative and myself on the day in question instead of merely reading the notes. She indicated that she would call me back within three days with an answer to whether or not the customer service representative recorded accurately my request. The time frame passed and I did not receive a response. Furthermore, I had to make a decision in regards to my mother's Christmas gift. If I did not receive the money back from T-Mobile and purchased the computer system, I was going to have insufficient funds for property taxes. I decided to purchase the adaptive computer that my mother needed in changing the lives of her students - despite my lack of money.

On New Year's Eve, my home church hosted one of my favorite Bible prophecy teachers, Perry Stone, who I assumed was going to deliver a dynamic message on the implications of current events on Biblical eschatology. I was somewhat disappointed in his message when the message involved receiving a breakthrough in "three days," based on David's transition from losing almost everything to gaining more than enough within seventy-two hours in the book of Chronicles. I didn't see the application of the message to my life until I attempted to pay my T-Mobile bill, when I was informed that there was no balance due by the automated system. I immediately called customer service to see why this was so and found that there had been an executive decision to credit my account with not only the amount that was taken from my checking account, but an amount in surplus that would equal three months of free phone service. The restoration of the funds was made exactly three days after the purchase of the computer system for my mother and her students.

The entire dilemma served as a prelude to a situation that soon arose in making the monetary figures involved in the cell phone pre-test miniscule in comparison to the next trial. The message which caused me to reflect back on the timeline and recognize that the entire situation was under control, out of my control, served as assurance that if I could trust God in restoration through minor trials, the major trials would work out despite my inability to see a physical resolution on the "chess board."

Stirring Giants

I received a letter between Christmas and New Year's of 2008 from St. Vincent's Medical Center. Doubting strongly that it was a Christmas greeting card, I reluctantly opened it. I was mortified at what I found inside. It was a bill for my prior August bi-annual pump maintenance appointment in the amount of $54,000. A charge of $54,000 was the amount I was responsible for if I did not have insurance. Prior bills covered by the "Cadillac" coverage of my insurance company had shown a charge of $14,575. Of that amount the insurance company paid all but $575, which was my responsibility.

This realization was compounded by a lay-off notice that I received on the ninth of January that was to take effect on February thirteenth. If this layoff were to occur, I was uninsured as of March first. My next pump refill date was scheduled for the twenty-first of January, and I was responsible for $575 of that bill. I decided to have the dosage decreased as much as possible prior to March first while I still had impeccable insurance. Unless I could find another position that offered incredibly comprehensive insurance benefits I'd be out of luck and stuck with a $54,000 bill.

The tri-partied composite of humans is spirit, soul, and body, where victorious Christian living depends on the body being subjected to the soul, which is ultimately held in check and controlled by the spirit man. However, it's incredibly difficult to take every thought into subjection, especially when a physical $54,000 bill is staring one in the face, and in addition has also just been informed that the next refill might not be covered by insurance at all. It seemed that Satan was primed and ready to complete the "Job"ification process in taking my house and the rest of my assets in a whirlwind of medical bills. I immediately started forming a contingency plan to get completely off the medicine prior to March.

I have occupied the thought of decreasing the level of medication before and have even suggested it in passing to my neurologist because of the out-of-control, skyrocketing inflation in the medical industry. I was never in the position of having to pull the plug — that is coming off my medication completely — until this point. My next refill was scheduled at the end of January; I was going to ask the pain management specialist to decrease my dosage by ten percent.

During my appointment at the Pain Management Clinic, I informed them of my game plan, telling them that I was aware that I had become chemically addicted to the drug and desired to start weaning myself off in ten percent increments starting on that day. The nurse then explained the semantical difference between addiction and dependence.

I retorted, "You're correct, being hooked on a drug that's more potent, expensive, and causes more exorbitant residual costs to the taxpayer was worse than addiction in that the user understands and detests the draining effects on society."

She went on to inform me that the pump adjustment entailed written instructions from my neurologist. This was not what I wanted to hear as this meant at least two more appointments.

I set up an appointment with Dr. Bauer, my neurologist, to establish a definitive schedule for reductions and asked him to fax the Pain Management Clinic an order to decrease the dosage at the maximum permissible rate. The next day, I received a call from Pain Management Clinic indicating that they had received the fax from Dr. Bauer who approved a five percent reduction. This was not what I had hoped, but better than nothing, so I made a trip to St. Vincent's confident of my ability to persuade them to "accidentally" take me down by more, which they denied. Years were necessary in weaning off the medication in five percent increments.

I went to my appointment with Dr. Bauer. After a twenty-minute, high-intensity, animated monologue in which a comprehensive, detailed analysis was clearly given in justification of my decision, he responded by stating, "Ernie, I fully understand and endorse your desire to get off this medication, but my job is to safely guide you through the process." He went on to say that he had never had a patient decrease the dosage on baclofen and had never heard of anybody completely coming off the medication after having been on such a high dosage for so long. I swallowed hard, remembering Dr. Cameron's warnings of the permanence of the decision and the threat that the spasms would "come back with a vengeance," if I ever substantially decreased doses.

I winced as I asked a realistic timeline in weaning off the drug, anticipating an unacceptably slow process. My hopes fell as he responded, "Well, a safe decrease schedule is five percent every three months." This nullified the notion of avoiding bankrupting medical charges if I was ever without impeccable insurance. I might as well not even bother with the decreases, just expect to lose everything and become a Medicaid junky. The stark reality of the impossible situation hit me when I asked what the potential side effects of a more aggressive reduction schedule were. There were three levels of withdrawal symptoms. The lowest level included high blood pressure, increased heart-rate, constipation, trouble urinating, and more; the intermediate symptoms were the possibility of major organ failure; and the greatest risk being death. He provided several medical journal articles, which graphically illustrated the prevalent risks. I never finished the first article as it started with a patient whose blood pressure was 215/155, pulse 118 beats per minute, all the major organs in a state of failure and extreme muscle spasticity due to baclofen withdrawal. This decision was a little more serious than I had originally thought and realized I needed the doctor's wisdom.

Cold turkey wasn't an option. If these were potential implications in reducing baclofen too quickly, my original plan was disastrous. I wasn't opposed to taking risks; I've done that my whole life and things always turned out for the better. Dr. Bauer did not dismiss the complete titration of baclofen dosage to independence, but recommended a second opinion be sought after by one of the leading experts in the field of baclofen pump maintenance at Cleveland Clinic.

The Spirit of Pharmacopoeia

Questions raged in my mind as to how and why I became hooked on such a powerful and destructive pharmaceutical that an attempt at breaking the dependence could be fatal, and by staying on the drug financial bankruptcy was imminent, where the combination of both yielded psychological unrest. I reflected on the circumstances surrounding the introduction of the drug in the first place as a suitable remedy in alleviating my anguish and how I initially had contested the idea of implanting a permanent device into my body until the doctor convinced me to try it out. At which time he administered a day's dose in the span of five seconds, which resulted in instantaneous addiction and bondage, followed by a pursuit of that ultimate euphoric effect which caused voluntary increases in dosage that compounded my situation. If I had the foresight of the long term consequences, I never would have agreed to the trial. Unaware of the astronomical cost of the medication combined with the dependence factor at the introduction of the baclofen pump, I now found myself in a quandary that was not quickly or easily resolved. There had to be an alternate explanation as to why this treatment had been used.

The phenomenon I was entangled in had been transcribed millennia ago in the book of Enoch, which pre-dates the book of Job, the oldest book of the Bible. The primary reason that the book of Enoch was omitted as a holy inspired text from the canonized scripture was lax transcription practices employed by Hebrew scribes in passing this ancient text down, which ultimately led to flawed translations. Aside from the fact that Hebrew rabbis, as well as church clergy, held this text in high regard and taught directly from Enoch until the third century A.D., several direct references from the Bible to the book of Enoch lend credibility to the historical accuracy of the text. First, Genesis 6 speaks of fallen angels or sons of God intermarrying with the daughters of men producing an offspring of giants that inhabited the earth that necessitated the deluge. Passages found in Joshua, Judges, 1 Samuel, and 1 Chronicles reference giants which further validate the book of Enoch. Secondly, one of the chief watcher's names over the two-hundred fallen angels who came down on Mount Herman was Azazel. The name Azazel was later given to the Passover scapegoat in Exodus by Moses, which was taken away from the camp and killed. At the precise moment in which Azazel's life-blood was cut off, a red ribbon that was mounted in the temple turned white indicating the remittance of sin. Lastly, the book of Jude takes a direct quote from the first chapter of the book of Enoch, "See, the Lord is coming with thousands upon thousands of his holy ones to judge everyone, and judge the ungodly for their ungodly acts..." (Jude 1:15,16), solidifying a rightful position of relevance of the book of Enoch in the study of history.

The book of Enoch indicates that Azazel assigned different areas of control to specific fallen angels or nephilum spirits. Eight specific areas are detailed in Enoch including the jurisdictions of murder, which is a spirit dispatched to convince people that the taking of a life is permissible; a spirit assigned to attack people's psyches through depressive thoughts; and another spirit with the assignment to teach man "the cutting of roots" which is equipping people with the knowledge of how to use organic plants in psycho-expanding recreational and medicinal drugs. Every one of these assigned areas apportioned thousands of years ago to demonic spirits as related in the account of Enoch are operable in the twenty-first century.

All pharmaceuticals are derivatives from the "knowledge in cutting of roots," which often times create more instability in conditions prior to treatment. For instance, a hindering spirit might be dispatched to aggravate someone, who in turn develops high blood pressure. Instead of utilizing biblical nutritional habits in decreasing the blood pressure, the person may obtain a prescription for regulatory medication, thereby permitting the spirit of pharmacopoeia to gain a foothold in their life. The analogy holds up when extended to encompass many more conditions, often times with severe consequences. A person suffering with a mild case of bi-polar disorder is often times offered a powerful psychotropic drug that opens the door for more voices to enter their head, leaving the person worse off than they were prior to the experiment. This is not an open ended condemnation of all pharmaceuticals. For example, if somebody is suffering from a severe stress headache, taking an aspirin may restore normal blood flow. However, if the pharmaceutical has negative side effects, even if the drug is itself benign, it is because the spirit of pharmacopoeia has attached itself to it.

This was exactly my situation; the spirit of pharmacopoeia entered into my life through a very potent drug, although the drug in itself was not demonic since there were no psychological, mental or other side effects. However, the negative psychological, external side effects of opening bills stating that I would owe tens of thousands of dollars to the hospitals if I ever became uninsured is most certainly connected to the Watcher that was granted authority by Azazel to hinder peoples' minds through fear and other psychological games. Responding to this fear caused me to actively pursue weaning myself off the drug that was responsible for the spirit of fear entering my life. This generated a negative report where words of death, and not life, were offered as a warning in attempting to remove the source of my negative emotions. In this way, three of the nephilum spirits, operating in the same capacity as delineated in Enoch, were working in concert to wreak havoc in my life. This illustrates Jesus' warning of cleaning one's house after He had cast a demon out of a person that if they permitted the demonic spirit to come back, the spirit brings more demons to take up residency. Likewise, the demon of pharmacopoeia was allowed in my life, under the pretense of "relieving spasticity" while having the intentions all along of opening the door to other conspirators under the guise of outrageous medical bills. House cleaning was in order, the kind that required supernatural intervention due to all the variables. It would also entail the same reckless abandon that I had as a child, the faith proceeding from a child that is confident of the divine protection of the Lord.

Slaying the Giants

The visible, conspiring factors giving license to the spirit of pharmacopoeia to manifest in a profound and overwhelming way were greed and overinflated costs of health care provision. First, the cycle of healthcare greed begins in pharmaceutical laboratories where millions of dollars are spent on developing a powerful drug that relieves spasticity. A salesman then markets the new drug to distributors, who find physicians to pedal the product. The neurologists, who already have a client base which "benefits" from this new drug, then convince them to undergo a trial. On trial day, the needle is loaded with the medication that gives the patient a euphoric relief never to be experienced again once the drug becomes a daily ritual. By the time the bill reaches the insurance company, the extremely exorbitant hospital bills are reduced and discounted. As long as the patient is gainfully employed or has good insurance, the employer pays the premium, steadily pumping a stream of revenue into a bureaucracy where no single person realizes how much a service costs except the person receiving the final statement from the insurance company.

As insurance companies decrease coverage and begin denying claims, or insurance is lost for whatever reason, the inevitable pitch for socialized medicine is made by the politicians, which is embraced by more and more people as they're made to look off the cliff into the valley of bankruptcy. It's a matter of degrees; not everybody is dependent on such a devastating drug should provision be denied. However, a skyrocketing amount of citizens are reliant on blood pressure, cholesterol, or other types of pharmaceuticals; they become accomplices in fabricating the case for socialized medicine and joining the ranks of the "Universalists." Although these two natural accelerants are powerful in themselves, their power over my life was to be broken when the source of their authority, the spirit of pharmacopoeia, was broken off my life.

Possessing the framework and justification as to why I had to get off the medication and having already initiated the consultations with the appropriate neurologists, I was convinced of the necessity of the action but very concerned of the prognosis that was given. Even if I were to successfully come off the medicine with minimal or no adverse side effects, the spasticity that was being masked for seven years was to return. I had no idea to what degree, but I knew that baclofen was very effective at what it was created to do, so when the inhibiter was removed and the flood gates were opened I may be worse off than I had been prior to the medication. My concerns were eased as I remembered reading of a Christian evangelist, Mel Tari, who was instructed by God to cross a river that had no bridge, permitting him to share the gospel with some un-evangelized people. Rather than questioning how they were going to get across the river without a bridge, he and his team obediently walked across the river to the other side. Likewise, I decided it was time to knock the baclofen bridge down and "walk on water."

One evening, as I watched an internet broadcast of Delores Winder's incredible testimony of her miraculous healing, God spoke to me directly through her. Kathryn Kuhlman stated that Delores Winder's healing was one of the most profound creative miracles of the twentieth century. Delores Winder agonizingly suffered with a bone condition in which her bones were literally dissolving for a period of over nineteen years. Pseudoartrosis is an incurable and extremely painful bone disease. Three different doctors diagnosed her as being terminal and authorized two percutaneous lobotomies, irreversible procedures where a neurosurgeon entered the back of her skull and burned the sensory neurons to eliminate her sense of feeling throughout the majority of her body. She was taking high doses of morphine to mitigate the remaining pain. After being given only days to live, she attended a Kathryn Kuhlman service. Her legs started to feel as though they were on fire. She informed a doctor that was sitting next to her of the sensation and also shared with him that she had two percutaneous lobotomies. He knew that it was impossible for her to feel anything having undergone such medical procedures. He knew she was receiving a miraculous work and took her to the front. As Kathryn Kuhlman prayed for her, she was totally healed instantaneously. At her next routine checkup with her primary physician, he could find no signs of her bone disease. He sat down and asked her to explain what had happened, as she had a clean bill of health which was quantifiably impossible due to her prior condition. He ended the appointment by inquiring about the amount of morphine that she was taking. She responded that she had stopped taking it as soon as she was healed! He responded by informing her that, in itself, was a miracle because anybody coming off the amount of morphine she had been taking cold turkey was going to experience convulsions and withdrawal. At that moment in the interview she turned to the television camera and informed the viewing audience that there was somebody who, "is on a medication that the doctor's have said that you can't live without." I had no question in my mind -- that was the confirmation necessary to confidently move ahead with my plan to get off the medication without fearing metabolic backlash.

I traveled to Cleveland, Ohio to consult with one of the nation's foremost experts in baclofen pumps, since my primary neurologist had never had a patient request reductions in their doses, let alone come off the medication completely. The primary purpose was not to discuss risks or the "proper way" of reduction, but rather to have him fax documentation to my neurologist to expedite the reductions at a greater rate than five percent every three months. The meeting went better than expected; there was not even a reference to the potential negative side effects of what I was desirous to do, but rather an attitude of patient discretion. He stated that, "I don't like to jump to conclusions, time will tell; just try reducing the rate and if you can tolerate it, that's great. If you can't you have the emergency pills so symptoms may be offset until you can get back in for an increase." The pills he was referring to were a supply of oral baclofen and a potent anti-anxiety muscle relaxant which my primary neurologist had prescribed when he authorized the Pain Clinic to begin reductions

He faxed over detailed instructions to my neurologist, who then forwarded them to St. Vincent's Pain Clinic and I was able to commence my reductions in kicking the habit. One of the restrictions indicated in the fax was that I was not permitted to reduce the medication more than twenty percent a week. I went in for another reduction ten days after the first twenty percent decrease and explained to the nurse, "I had absolutely no side effects whatsoever after the twenty percent reduction." I elaborated, "I had mild discomfort after the five percent reduction a month ago. The difference was the word of knowledge that I received between then and now from Delores Winder." I went on to share Delores Winder's story.

She said she appreciated my level of faith, but there was too much paperwork if something went wrong. She was obligated to stick to the prescribed schedule, so I went down another twenty percent.

The next visit entailed a change in potency of the medication to a quarter of the prior amount. I wasn't very enthused about this development as it entailed another "surgical procedure" costing the insurance company thousands of dollars and me hundreds. She said that it was a necessary step because, "Although you nearly cut the doses in half, it's still very concentrated and you're still getting a lot of benefit from the medication."

I replied, "So it's like going from heroin to morphine!"

She said, "Yes," as she plunged the needle into the pump. I made a few more visits in a relatively short period of time, and the pump was administering the lowest possible dose without being turned off. Instead of turning the device directly off, the weaning procedure mandated putting saline solution in the device until it was confirmed that I did not need the medication any longer. I had been told that once the pump was turned off, it was not possible to restart. The injection of the saline solution entailed another costly surgical procedure.

After I had successfully weaned myself off the medication completely, I looked forward to the day when I would undergo surgery once again to remove the pump. This time there was no replacement system; when the device was taken out I was free of the hindrance, which it had become. The pump itself wasn't bothersome; it merely looked as if a hockey puck was lodged in my lower left abdominal region. It was the catheter, which ran from the device to fuse with my spinal chord that caused discomfort. On account of my active lifestyle, the catheter was jarred and moved around which was adjustable when I contorted my back. This led to many sleepless nights as I tossed and turned, trying to position it back into place. I finally had an opportunity to rid myself of this painful problem, a secondary benefit of getting off baclofen.

The procedure itself wasn't cumbersome. The surgery took under an hour where the surgeon cut along the same scar tissue that was left from my prior surgeries, disconnected the catheter from the pump and removed the device. They then turned me over backside up and made the smaller incision to access my spinal chord, at which point the catheter was disconnected and removed. They then sewed me back up and waited for me to wake up from the anesthesia. At that point the recovery phase began where I had to lie completely flat on my back for a few days. As with my prior surgeries, I fully recovered within a week raring to go.

There is a time in every situation when God will act to prevent those who call upon His name from falling into a situation that they cannot tolerate. I was faced with a situation in which there were two options from the natural perspective. First, continue racking up medical bills, forfeit assets and salary until income was less than that of the federal poverty level and become dependent on Medicaid to provide a medication that eases symptoms of a very uncomfortable neurological abnormality. Secondly, cut the medication, eliminating the need to fret over bills but have serious withdrawal implications, followed by the resumption of an equal or greater level of spasticity than prior to utilization of the medication to mitigate the symptoms. In either case, the conclusive results from a physical standpoint were not permitted by a God who wants only good for his children. That's the reason for the baffling results of weaning myself off the medication without any adverse side effects, and without a return of super-spastic symptoms, both of which were physiologically impossible from a medical standpoint according to neuro-experts and empirical medical research.

I've often pondered why God is allowing my physical maladies to fester for so long without performing the creative miracles that He is known for in the Bible. These miracles have been duplicated throughout the ages, serving as signs and wonders, demonstrating the unmistakable power of God. Just as God has dispatched guardian angels to protect me throughout my life, He has also held true to all of His promises in the Holy Scriptures that are guaranteed to all who put their trust and confidence in Christ Jesus. Throughout my life, I have had confidence to entrust my eternal soul to the care of the Father through the acceptance of Jesus' sacrifice on the cross, and I can be absolutely confident that the same cross of salvation will also bring complete physical healing in my life. The trigger event for becoming independent from medication, my layoff notice (which as of this writing has not taken effect), served as a means to increase my faith in God and stop relying on the medications of man which were unable to heal my body. Our conceptualization of time inhibits our ability to understand why physical manifestations of healing aren't instantaneous. While one is waiting for the manifestation of a miracle, it's pertinent to be tried, tested and approved; not as a precondition for receipt of a miracle, but for the purpose of humbling oneself so that when the miracle is manifested, they will give it back to the Lord as an offering tried by fire.

Part 3
Divine Destiny

Chapter 12

Life's Purpose

The three foremost questions in the mind of a person is searching for reason and meaning in life are: why are we here, what is the purpose of life, and what happens after we die? These questions demand cogent answers, especially for anybody whose extraordinary circumstances create the illusion of meaninglessness. In fact, if I concluded, based on my condition as an early teen that my visual impairment and neurological disorder was attributable to random chance, then evolution and survival of the fittest satisfied the first of the three questions. A resolution that if I was not the fittest, then survival and competition in a world demanding physical perfection leading to hopelessness was the inevitable response to the question. If this was my final conclusion to the first question, then the second and third ones were irrelevant. If everything is a product of random chance, there is no purpose in life and no final destination after death. I am a rational being so I desired to objectively determine the true answers. Everybody has personal bias; they have a predisposition which automatically places them on a point of the spectrum prior to analysis of the facts. However, they will gravitate toward the truth providing they are intellectually honest.

Reason for Being

"Where did we come from?" This is a question that has two mutually exclusive answers. Either everything evolved over millions of years as I was taught in public schools, or everything was created in a seven day week, according to the creation account of the Bible. Evolutionists have a presupposition that if a natural explanation satisfies a particular question, the possibility of a supernatural explanation is eliminated. In this vein, the "Big Bang" is placed over 6.5 billion years ago with the explanation that everything will occur naturally if enough time transpires. Meanwhile, carbon isotope dating, as well as other flawed measurement standards, is used to date "geological eras" and "fossil chains," undergirding their preconceived foundational principle that everything came from nothing, which ultimately entails more faith than taking the creation account at face value. Statistically speaking, it's more probable for somebody to put diamonds, gold, glass, tiny screws, and gears in a shoe-box, shake it up for a thousand years, and upon opening the box to find a perfectly engineered, ticking Rolex watch set to the appropriate time.

It is as equally irresponsible to base faith in creation in ignorance. There is compelling anthropological, geological, and historical evidence supporting creation while disproving evolution. For instance, a fossilized leg of a Tyrannosaurus Rex was found in California complete with blood vessels and soft tissue intact. A tree was found fossilized vertically, within several rock layers, which, according to evolutionists, each rock layer is formed over millions of years. If the fossilization process took hundreds of thousands of years, the preservation of soft organic matter is impossible indicating that fossils form much faster than evolutionists admit. The Bible records a massive geological event, accounting for the accelerated fossilization of the majority of the fossil record, captured in the flood recorded in Genesis 6. This phenomenon is not unique to Christians and the Bible; most major and minor religions have a deluge account where the "Supreme Being" sent a flood to wipe out all humanity because of perpetual evil. In addition to this, cultures, even prior to the influence of Christian missionaries, have legends of a great flood indicating that the flood is not an allegorical concoction intended to strike fear and awe in people of a divine creator for manipulation purposes, but an actual historical event.

An exhaustive evaluation of the evidence in proving creation is the only explanation as to why we are here entails much research, and in doing so a skeptic will find that the above referenced examples aren't anecdotal. Ken Ham of Answers in Genesis Ministries and Henry Morris have devoted their lives to studying creation from a Biblical standpoint and have determined through thousands of hours of research, as well as through the writing of many books and other tools, that the Bible is consistently flawless in its accuracy of the creation account. The Creation Museum in Kentucky has been established; it exhibits in a literal format the 6,000 years of history of the world. Various ministries have websites, (www.answersingenesis .com), debunking the theories of secular humanism utilizing the truth of the Bible. When everything is considered, the facts fall squarely on the side of creationism. If that conclusion is not embraced, then it is a matter of pride that prevents a person in accepting that there is a God in Heaven.

The Sole Purpose in Life

After one realizes that everything was created by a Supreme Being, the second question necessitating an answer is, "For what purpose were we created?" This answer can be reached through philosophical gymnastics and logical reasoning which many writers have already written on. If the reader is dissatisfied with the brief overview of this defense of Christianity, they are encouraged to read the writings of C.S. Lewis, a self-proclaimed atheist who arrived at the realization of Jesus Christ as the only means of salvation after knowing that if he were to maintain objectivity, he must consider Christianity as a plausible world view and in doing so he realized the divinity of Christ. Another prolific writer in the arena of Christian apologetics is Ravi Zacharias who was born into a Hindu Pantheistic culture and found the truth of Christ Jesus on a bed of suicide. He then devoted his life to the defense of the Christian faith by debating the world's most renowned atheists, Buddhists, Hindus, and foremost experts in New Age philosophy.

The starting point in determining which religion or world view

197

comprehensively delineates morality is pertinent in determining the correct line of thought in defining one's purpose. Morality cannot be relative. Everyone agrees that a person who violently sexually assaults and murders a young child has perpetrated an evil act. Since there is evil in the world, then it logically follows that there is good. Furthermore, there must be absolute good and absolute evil providing the framework for defining morality. A moral code is necessary in placing a deed on the spectrum of good or evil. Lastly, there must be a moral law giver, who is inclusively absolutely good, capable of defining the moral code. Thus we arrive at the conclusion that there must be an absolutely good, divine being in existence based on nothing more than the observation that evil exists in our world.

A problematic situation arose when man thought that he was capable of understanding the moral code. The only command given to Adam in the Garden of Eden was, "... of every tree of the garden thou mayest freely eat; but of the tree of the knowledge of good and evil, thou shalt not eat of it" (Gen 2:16, 17). At the moment this commandment was violated, man's eyes of moral judgment were opened. The next generation from Adam witnessed the first murder, and ever since mankind has digressed into moral relativism where the parameters of right and wrong are calibrated according to mortal conceptualization of good and evil. Prior to consumption of the fruit from the tree of knowledge, man did not have to worry about breaking a moral law because he did not distinguish between good and evil. In their innocence, Adam and Eve had no option but to do good, until the knowledge of good and evil entered their minds, subjecting all humanity to evil. It is not a matter of degrees — a little poop in the brownies taints the entire batch. Likewise, the concentration of evil in the world was irrelevant as redemptive measures were necessary to restore humanity after the conferring of the knowledge of good and evil.

Immediately, God established a redemptive plan prophetically recorded in Genesis 3:15, "And I will put enmity between thee and the woman, and between thy seed and her seed; it shall bruise thy head and thou shalt bruise His heel." This prophecy was fulfilled about 4,000 years after the Garden of Eden, yet incremental steps toward a fully redemptive covenant were made during the interim. An everlasting covenant was made between God and the Hebrew people as recorded in Exodus. A covenant was made during Moses' ascent of Mount Sinai to receive the Torah, God's written law. Accompanying the written law was an oral law and sacrificial feasts and celebrations, which served as commemorations of historical events and consecration for the sins of the Israelites. Animal sacrifices were offered on the Day of Atonement in the fall covering the sins of the Israelites from the previous year. A spotless, white lamb was also sacrificed on the day of Passover in the spring in commemoration of God ushering the Israelites out of Egypt. The blood of animals, however, was temporal and limited in their redemptive qualities, only allowing forgiveness once a year.

This, coupled with the inability for mere mortal man to adhere completely to the law given to Moses, caused God to graciously assume physical flesh as Jesus Christ. He **"walked among men, being temped in all ways, yet without sin,"** and **literally "became sin" as an all sufficient and spotless sacrifice,** thus fulfilling all of the Old Testament prophecies regarding His first advent and establishing the New Covenant which provides access to the kingdom of God for all people. Jesus' resurrection, His final redemptive act, was the exact fulfillment of three hundred thirteen Old Testament prophecies, which when subjected to statistical laws far exceed the threshold of an occurrence happening by random chance, meaning the prophecies fulfillment by Jesus' life did not happen by chance. In other words, Jesus' virgin birth, His ministry while on Earth, his death, burial, and resurrection occurred with such precision as foretold in a time span of 1,500 to 400 years prior to His birth in the Old Testament, that there is no possibility that the events happened by chance.

God unconditionally honors His covenants as evidenced by the Jewish people today. No other people group has been systematically persecuted throughout history, from the enslavement of the Hebrews around 1585 BC in Egypt, after being established as a nation by God of their exile to Babylon in 606 BC, to the Roman persecutions in the second uprooting of Israel as a nation in 70 AD, to the expulsion of Jews from Great Britain during the 13th century and from Spain in 1492, and most recently to Hitler's Holocaust. In 1948 they were restored as a sovereign nation in "a single day" as predicted in the Psalms and by the prophets of the Bible. No people group has been uprooted twice from the same geographical region, to be replanted in the exact locality 3,500 years after their original establishment. Furthermore, the Jewish population comprises 1% of the world's population, yet 32% of the world's millionaires are Jewish. An everlasting covenant between God and Abraham is the only explanation as to why such blessing and prosperity has been bestowed upon the Jewish people. If God still honors the first covenant He made with a small people group, we can be confident that He'll honor the second and better covenant that was made with the entire world.

The purpose in God establishing covenants with mankind stem from His desire to have a created family that will commune with Him for eternity. He first created the angels for this purpose, and one third of them fell, following Satan when he desired to be God's superior in authority and dominion. Subsequently, God created man to do what these angels failed to do — to be content to praise and worship God in holy communion in a familial relationship as sons and daughters in a royal family. As with the angels, man fell when he was deceived into thinking that he could become like God and possess the knowledge between good and evil in determining his own moral code. Despite this fallen condition, God had a plan to draw all man back unto Himself, starting first with the house of Israel, and then the entire world.

Reality of Eternity

The previous two sections discussed the two premiere stumbling blocks which Satan utilizes to convince people to reject the Christian faith. A third deceptive perpetration that Satan uses in causing people to question the literal interpretation of the Bible is the anti-doctrine of the existence of a literal Hell. The classical argument is that if the God of the Bible is an all-loving and an all-forgiving God, then how can He send people to Hell? A concise answer is that God is a Spiritual Being who cannot cohabitate with sin. This violates a spiritual principle that He established. In other words, absolute good cannot exist with evil. God dwells in Heaven, a place defined as absolute good. He cannot allow any evil whatsoever to dwell with Him without violating a spiritual principle. So if sin has not been covered and excused in one's life prior to their spirit's departure from this physical world into the next, their spirit must go somewhere for eternity. The alternative to Heaven is Hell. This reasoning is abstract without supportive evidence. The Bible is consistent in the concept of eternity and every person will spend it in either Heaven or Hell. Still extra-biblical accounts aide in convincing skeptics that these places are a reality.

Dr. Maurice Rawlings, an atheistic cardiologist, was performing a routine stress test on one of his patients in the 1970s. As he observed his patient walking on the treadmill, the man suddenly collapsed. Dr. Rawlings immediately started chest compressions to keep the man's heart beating. When he paused to attempt to put a tourniquet around the patient's arm, his heart stopped beating. Dr. Rawlings resumed compressions, which re-started the patient's heart who exclaimed that he "was in Hell" and to "please save me." Whenever Dr. Rawlings postponed the chest compressions, the patient's heart stopped and everything was quiet. As soon as Dr. Rawlings started compressions, the patient revived with the same screams of being in Hell and to save him. Dr. Rawlings advised the patient to keep his Hell to himself and that he was a doctor trying to save his life, not a priest. Eventually Dr. Rawling's nurse asked him to do something as she observed that the patient was in agony. It was at this point that Dr. Rawlings asked the patient to repeat his statements. Dr. Rawlings admitted that he did not know how to pray, but the sinners' prayer that he led his patient in included the essentials of recognizing that he was a sinner and for Jesus to come into his heart. After this, the next time the patient was revived from unconsciousness, a calm and serene countenance was upon his face. The patient's life was ultimately saved and he later recounted in detail the account of literally experiencing Hell during the intermittent periods when his heart stopped beating. Dr. Rawlings accepted Jesus Christ as his savior due to that experience, discarding his cerebral world view.

He spent a considerable portion of his practice after his conversion medically researching and detailing near death experiences and what happens to people after they're clinically dead. His research focused on gathering and detailing cases where a person had been declared clinically dead. This is where a person's heart stops beating for six seconds and all oxygen stops flowing to the brain, at which point rigor mortis sets in. Medically documenting the cause of death for certain individuals, and the subsequent circumstances surrounding the restoration of life, he compiled evidence. Detailing the experiences of the various patients between dying and coming back to life from first hand interviews, Dr. Rawlings produced books detailing the accounts from a physician's standpoint, including "To Hell and Back." He found that upon death, people are immediately transported to one of two places: Heaven or Hell. He also concluded that fewer people who've seen an experienced Hell recount it for two reasons. First, they don't want to admit that they failed to make the correct decision on earth, which results in admission into Heaven, and secondly, the mortal mind is incapable of quantifying the horrific reality of a Hell experience thereby instantly mitigating or erasing the memory as a coping mechanism.

Bill Wiese experienced the horrors of Hell and recounts the experience in his book 23 Minutes in Hell. Bill and his wife returned from a Bible study and went to bed. At 3:00AM he was hurtled out of his body and landed on the floor of a cell cage in an environment that was so hot that he questioned how he was still alive due to the searing heat as well as water deprivation. Two thirteen foot tall creatures, which he describes in vivid detail, entered the cell with him and immediately started to shred the flesh off of his body, which regenerated, only to be brutally and perpetually torn off again. He explained that his spirit was separated from his physical body on earth, and placed into another physical body of anguish in Hell. He was transported out of the cage and placed next to a lake of fire where he observed the terrors of Hell, and later detailed them in his book with extensive cross references to the Bible.

He noted that his sensory perception in the spirit realm was more acute, amplifying the agony; his carnal desires were never again to be satisfied, and his regrets of past unjust acts that he committed on earth that were non-correctable rushed through his mind. He continuously thought of his wife and people above on the earth who had no idea what was transpiring with him beneath the earth. After what seemed like an eternity to him, he felt himself being pulled and lifted out of the putrid place. As he ascended through a tunnel, creatures, which were bound to the walls with chains, clawed at him. He continued to rise into outerspace where he observed earth and Jesus met with him face to face to inform him why he was sent to Hell for a glimpse. His recollection of being a Christian while on earth was erased to experience Hell as an unbeliever. His charge was to inform non-Christians that Hell is real and it is eternal if one dies without accepting Jesus as their Savior. He was permitted to briefly experience the literal Hell due to people ignoring the warnings in the Bible of the reality of the place. Even though Bill Wiese believes that the degree of duress and torment was limited, the psychological aftermath was such that it was months before he was able to discuss the experience. He spoke with Mary K. Baxter, another individual selected by God to inform a blissfully ignorant population of the reality of Hell, who advised him that it would take a year or so before mental recovery, and even then the reality of the experience was going to have a permanent effect.

Jesus came to Mary K. Baxter in a vision and advised her that he was going to escort her through Hell every night for thirty nights. Hell is a physical place situated deep inside the earth, as recorded in the Bible, and it's laid out like a person. Jesus took her through the left and right legs and arms of Hell, where she witnessed mourning, weeping, gnashing of teeth, and literal manifestations of the afflictions that define Hell in the Bible, including worms that continually eat the flesh of people, fire that is unquenchable and perpetual torment of people by demonic beings. She witnessed people who were trapped in cells, as Bill Wiese was, and the lake of fire, which he also saw. She also saw the body of Hell, where Satan's throne is located with the fallen angels or demons around it, attempting to replicate the Heavenly throne room.

She also saw people who were burning in pits and as Jesus and she approached, they recounted their life's story while on earth. She saw people who were wealthy before they died on earth, but the pursuit of earthly riches became their god and they ignored the true God. She saw people who she recognized as famous movie stars who worshiped the god of fame. She also saw a person who identified herself as being an ancient queen of a very powerful earthly kingdom who indicated that had she known the reality of Hell, she would have exchanged her earthly kingdom for the Heavenly one. One pit contained a man with his hands outstretched as if he was holding a Bible and quoting scripture as if he was teaching. He questioned Jesus why he was in Hell, to which Jesus replied that he did not teach the truth. At that point other people started berating and scorning the false preacher saying, "We followed you and you told us that there was no Hell!" Every person understood why they were in Hell and pleaded with Mary K. Baxter, as they knew she was not staying in Hell, to warn people that they still had time on earth to repent as there is no escape from this torment. After the thirty days, Jesus showed Mary K. Baxter a glimpse of Heaven and charged her with a similar responsibility as Bill Wiese. She was to tell the entire world that Hell is real, and especially the Christians who have adopted a notion that there is no Hell.

Earthquake Kelley, an Olympic Boxer in 1983, was born into a fifth generation Voodoo witchdoctor family on his father's side. His mother was a God-fearing Christian whose prayers were responsible for saving her son from certain destruction. His compelling autobiography, Born to Lose, Destined to Win, chronicles his life story, and powerfully validates the existence of Heaven and Hell.

He was just four years old when he started his witchcraft training. He began by placing curses on people and death was the result. He started using drugs at the age of five and was being prepared to practice witchcraft under Francois (Papa Doc) Duvalier, the Haitian governmental leader who controlled the country through

Voodoo. Kelley's life growing up consisted of peddling drugs, pimping prostitutes and consorting with spirits in pronouncing curses over people. Two of his friends accepted Jesus Christ as their personal Savior one day. It was a decision that Kelley didn't approve of, so he ordered two spirits to disrupt his friends' lives in order to convince them that they had made a wrong decision. The two spirits returned twice to Kelley informing him that they had no power to influence the boys. These spirits had successfully completed many assignments in the past, and he grew frustrated at the spirits' inability to inhibit the boys. Therefore, Kelley astro-projected out of his body to view the boys to gain insight as to what was obstructing his curse. Being able to look into the spirit realm Kelley saw his two recently Christianized friends, and they were surrounded by several eight-foot tall angels with flaming swords. He then realized that his friends had something more powerful than what he had and ceased placing curses on them.

One day when he was fifteen years old, his spirit guides instructed him how to get "super high." They told him to take high doses of crack cocaine, marijuana, a very potent hallucinogenic, and beer. The combination and amount of the drugs caused him to overdose and he died in the back seat of a car while he was being driven home. Immediately, the spirits that he had consorted with his entire life revealed themselves as demons. They rushed to his body and snatched his spirit from his body and started dragging him down into a pit. They informed him that it had been a trick to take his life and now he was theirs for eternity to torment and torture as they pleased. It's important to note at this juncture that he had no presupposition to a concept of Hell. In other words, his experience was not based on a subconscious belief in Hell, disproving the skeptics' charge of a temporal psychological experience based on an engraved belief system.

During his descent the demons clawed at him, and then he felt himself begin to rise, and heard the demons screaming that he was theirs and could not return to life. The next thing Kelley knew, he was back in his body and his friends in the car, thinking he was dead, pushed him out onto the street. He crawled to his porch and his sister helped him into their house realizing that he had overdosed. Despite his experience in Hell, after his recovery he reverted to selling drugs and his old habits. He appeased his sister by attending a church service. The second time he attended the church, the preacher singled him out from the back and called him to the front stating that God had a word for him. After walking to the front, the pastor proceeded to recount Kelley's entire life's story through the gift of knowledge given by the Holy Spirit, which perplexed Kelley. After hearing his biographical information recited by a complete stranger with a direct word that Jesus' sacrifice was sufficient to cover all of his sins, he accepted Christ as his personal Savior.

Later in life, Earthquake Kelley had surgery for a brain aneurism, resulting from his boxing career. He died while on the operating table, but this time he went to Heaven. In Heaven he saw his son on the opposite side of the river who had been killed in a gang related carjacking. Earthquake Kelley expressed his desire to cross the river to embrace his son, which was not allowed. However, he was permitted to converse with his son and his son reminded him that he had made a promise to continue helping people in need back on Earth and that his life's work was not complete. He was shown other things in Heaven by an angel that has been explicitly detailed in his book.

Conclusion

After examining the facts, an inquiry into life's fundamental question of the reason, purpose, and meaning of life show that everything in existence was created by an Infinite Being and did not evolve from primordial soup. The Christian faith is exclusively the way in which man enters back into a covenant with his Maker, thereby securing salvation. Heaven and Hell are literal, physical places. Exhaustive research into the validity of these three conclusions will find the intellectually honest researcher more convinced of the truth.

Although I encourage an intellectual framework in basing major decisions, there is a finite amount of time in making this decision. Nobody knows when their time in this world will come to a close, so don't overanalyze this decision, as pride often masquerades as rationalization. Facts are objective and are not subject to change if somebody determines to deny the truth because it doesn't neatly fit into their "ideal world view." If no other persuasive argument succeeds in prodding you into accepting the truth for what it is, remember that if Christians are right, then all alternatives are wrong, and whoever is not a Christian has an eternity of regret. So with this, three constants remain:

"All have sinned and fallen short of the glory of God." (Romans 3:23)

Every single person who has ever lived on the face of the Earth has committed evil acts that are not within the parameters established by God as being good. After God finished creating each segment of creation He said, "It is good," meaning perfect, without sin, and flawless. As soon as the first act outside of what God defined as good was committed, evil and sin entered into the genetic code of humanity extending to all people — everybody is subject.

"The wages of sin is death, but the free gift of God is Eternal life." (Romans 6:23)

The consequence of sin is death and eternal separation from the glory of God. Yet, God has extended an opportunity to live forever in communion with Him.

"For God so loved the world that He gave His only Begotten Son that whosoever believeth in Him shall not perish but have everlasting life." (John 3:16)

When God created the Heavens and the Earth it was perfect, flawless, and without sin. After man's disobedience by eating the forbidden fruit, sin corrupted creation. Since God loved and desired a relationship with His creation for eternity, the sinner has to be redeemed prior to restoration of the union. Blood sacrifice of animals, which temporarily remitted sin, was replaced by a second and lasting covenant which permanently remitted the sins of all those who believe. This spotless sacrificial lamb was Jesus Christ, God's only Son.

Prayer of Repentance

Dear Heavenly Father, I recognize that I am a sinner and have a sinful nature, preventing me from eternal communion with You. Thank You for sending Your Son, Jesus Christ, to bear all my sins and to become the ultimate sacrifice, permitting me to enter into an eternal relationship with You. Please equip me with the power and authority that Jesus promised to all who follow Him. Send the Holy Spirit to empower me to live in success and prosperity and to serve as a witness of the redemptive power of Christ. Thank you for saving me. Reveal Yourself more and more as I learn to walk in Your ways.

Epilogue

Miracles have been commonplace in my life, evidenced by the fullness and richness of the blessings bestowed on my life at such a young age. Quantification of the motivating factors driving the pursuit of prosperity, wholeness, and happiness in my life is not feasible outside of the hope found in the Lord Jesus Christ. This hope is brought to life every time a physical barrier is surmounted despite conditions that are not conducive for prosperity. We are engaged in one war having both spiritual and physical components. When Satan loses a spiritual battle, his physical assaults are intended to bring discouragement and loss of a spiritual battle through physical strife. God delights when His children prosper throughout their trials, tribulations, and afflictions wrought by the enemy and will provide an adequate level of grace and perseverance to overcome all assaults of the enemy.

The sole purpose in life after one makes a personal decision to accept Jesus Christ as their personal savior is to, "go ye into all the world and preach the gospel to every creature" (Mark 16:15). This most pertinent command is the strongest motivating factor for all Christians to live a righteous life. Everything we do is to be performed with "JOY," showing Jesus to Others through Yourself! If others cannot see Jesus through your actions, then they aren't being performed as an adequate testament to Jesus' grace and love. The most effective level of witnessing is reached when a non-believer's observations of a Christian's response to the trials and tribulations of this world leads them to salvation. As a non-believer ponders how a Christian overcomes tremendous difficulties to live a prosperous life, they will have no other option but to conclude that Christ is the only sufficient provider in this world.

Just as Paul did, we are to "glory in tribulations" (Romans 5:3). In doing so the message of Christ is conveyed more strongly than through intellectual reasoning. When people see that Jesus is alive and personally experienced in a Christian's life, apologetics becomes secondary. Everyone must study and be prepared to give an answer to all honest inquiries, but always be cognizant that their personal testimony is the most effective and primary tool for winning souls.

Life is limited to seventy to ninety years in length in most cases. This means two different things depending on where one stands; for the non-believer, it means they have the remainder of their life to find the only source of salvation. For the believer, the balance of their life is for them to spend it ushering unsaved people into the kingdom of God. An old hymnal states that this life will soon be past and only what is done for Christ will last. Christians sometimes lose sight of the primary objective and pray for personal success, healing, or deliverance from a particular situation when it might be the case that external witnesses to that struggle may be more positively influenced based on their observations than if deliverance was granted. Just as there is a seventy to ninety year window of opportunity for people to make a decision for Christ, that timeframe also limits the endurance of afflictions. If one finds himself under heavy assault from Satan, he is to realize that it's because he is attempting to prohibit you from maximum promulgation of the gospel.

So with this I exhort you to let your life shine for Christ in declaring his grace and sufficiency until we meet our Savior Jesus Christ in glory.

God has blessed me with an incredible ability to memorize and recall massive amounts of information. This is an ability and not a gift because it is not exclusive to myself. As I mentioned in my book that the ability was cultivated and enhanced through discipline, concentration and focus. This ability can and should be developed by everybody. Recall ability is important in committing the Bible to memory. This is why I assembled a very effective and comprehensive teaching in memorizing the Bible. It consist of the following five elements:

1. Understanding how God created us
2. A concise & comprehensive understanding of the physiology & neuro-anatomy of the brain
3. An understanding of working memory
4. Applying mnemonic devices & conversion of short-term memory into long-term memory
5. Methodology & demonstrations

Please visit my website for more information in obtaining this teaching or on how to contact me for speaking engagements.

www.ernieberry.com